That Undeniable Longing

THAT UNDENIABLE LONGING

My Road to and From the Priesthood

MARK TEDESCO

ACADEMY CHICAGO PUBLISHERS

Published in 2006 by
Academy Chicago Publishers
363 West Erie Street
Chicago, Illinois 60610

First paperback edition 2010

Printed and bound in the U.S.A.

Library of Congress Cataloging-in-Publication Data on file
with the publisher

ISBN: 978-0-89733-599-7

"In the end we will all be judged by how much we have loved"
—*St. John of the Cross*

Contents

———

What Lies Beyond

———

As I lay awake at night flooded with thoughts of the past, I wonder if this is what happens in middle age: memories become as important as the present, and in old age they become even more important. How did I arrive at this point? Could I ever have imagined, long ago on a winter day in Rome, that I would find myself on this new path, my dreams not shattered, but transformed. And that elusive, relentless desire, for happiness—where is it leading me? I ask myself this as day breaks and begins to illuminate the clouds below my window. Why is the question: "Am I happy?" so puzzling? Happy compared with what? Sad compared with what? The questions turn into dreams and dancing images as I drift into sleep.

———

"Our descent has begun into Rome," the loudspeaker blasts. "We're almost there!" Mike cries excitedly; "I can't wait to see the city again: the Forum, the museums, the Vatican! I would like to go out to Tivoli this time to see Hadrian's Villa. I was there years ago. And I remember an odd-looking modern church across the freeway; someone told me it's worth seeing. It's in a place called San Vittorino. Have you been out there?"

"San Vittorino." What strange feelings that name evokes. "Yes," I reply, "years ago. Sure, we can do that."

As we disembarked and went through customs and looked for a ride into the city, I felt myself back again in 1978 when I found Rome, or Rome found me. *"Buon Natale, signore!"* I had been surrounded by women in bright skirts, holding signs that said "Merry Christmas," pressing the signs against my body. They were gypsies,

"Buon Natale, signore, la vuole?" One smiled at me. My Italian was good enough, even then at 18 years old, that I could guess they were offering me a girl. I felt probing hands underneath the signs, searching my pockets. I pulled back in anger and raised my fist at them. They backed off, looking hurt, as if to say, "But *signore*, we only wanted to wish you a Merry Christmas and welcome you to this place by helping you to carry your money. We only wanted to help you and you dare to suspect us of wanting only your money! *You* are the terrible one!"

The gypsies constituted my welcoming committee that first time in Europe, but they could not spoil the experience. When I stood next to the Roman Forum, I imagined the ancient bustling *Via Sacra*: senators walking out of the senate house disagreeing about policy, exotic animals being led down a side road to be sold, slaves and other foreigners speaking in dozens of languages, an orator spouting off eloquent nothings before a small crowd. I could almost hear it among the chatting of tourists.

Behind me, next to the Forum, was the Mamertine prison; a cistern that in ancient times was used as a handy jail or holding cell. There is a legend that St. Peter himself was held there, as was St. Paul at a later date. To commemorate this belief, an altar has been built in the cell. On the floor of the cell is a hole, water bubbles up in it from an underground spring. Since in Rome every phenomenon has a story attached to it, this spring was said to have bubbled to the surface as St. Peter looked for water to baptize his Roman guard. As the guide explained this, I listened in wide-eyed amazement, excited to be here.

My friend Marcus and I had been invited to come to Rome by an American priest who had visited us in high school. He was traveling though the U.S. interviewing those interested in studying for the priesthood at San Vittorino. Now here we were—18 years old, and in Rome! The city of contradictions and magic, in which the impossible becomes possible! Even the street corners seem to speak: testaments to miracles, laws of nature suspended, magic woven into everyday life.

"Mark," Marcus called, "hurry up, we have to go!" He and I had been in high school together and now we were in our first year at college. Marcus, who had a light complexion and dark hair, had been adopted into a close-knit Hispanic family, and was the center of attention whenever I visited his home. His mother, aunts and uncles all doted on him. His older brother had moved out and started his own family. In high school I had envied Marcus, wishing I had a family like his. They tried to give him anything he needed or even just wanted. This did not necessarily turn out well for him. He became used to getting his own way; a state of mind that was to create difficulties for him when he was an adult.

Marcus and I had very different personalities and backgrounds, but we shared a passionate interest in the Catholic Church. My interest began at the age of fourteen when my mother died. Death can cause a child to focus on meaning, on a search for the unchanging; it can reveal the superficiality of those things that fill one's horizon. Marcus's interest lay in Catholic culture, history and liturgy, of which I knew practically nothing. But we had come together to this city of magic.

As we boarded the van to take us to the seminary in San Vittorino, I told Marcus about my encounter with the Roman gypsies, but he didn't seem much interested. We had come to this city in anticipation of a dream, mostly mine, of visiting a seminary to get a taste of that life, to perhaps begin the long road to the priesthood. At that point we were interested more in the seminary than in the priesthood itself, which seemed hazy and distant.

Our van navigated the narrow streets, cutting off other cars, speeding through several lights, brushing two pedestrians. I caught my breath as I spotted the Coliseum in the distance. I could almost hear the roar of spectators cheering their favorite gladiator as he made his entrance, booing as his opponent entered. It was winter and Rome seemed much grayer than American cities, but it was a majestic gray with the weight of history filling each stone with life. We careened through the residential section where I saw more apartment buildings in one place than I had ever seen. We followed the raised freeway and then left the city completely as we sailed onto the highway, green hills whirling by.

At the brick-and-cement seminary, several men were standing in the front yard, chatting before lunch. One, Chuck, was particularly friendly. He came up to greet us and we settled into a conversation before we entered the building. He was a jolly dark-haired man with a thick Boston accent, a quick smile and an easy laugh. He was in his second year at the seminary in San Vittorino.

When I asked him why he had come there, he said, "I wanted a solid seminary, and of course, there's Brother Luigino." This obscure seminary outside Rome was filled with Americans because word had gotten around that it was a good seminary and its added benefit was the resident saint, Brother Luigino.

What constituted a "good seminary" for most of the men, was a place free of the divisive ideological battles going on in many American Catholic institutions at that time. All of us had heard the stories: groups pitted against each other, one side branding the other as "liberals" who were distorting the Catholic identity; the other side calling their enemies pre-Vatican II "conservatives." Each group considered itself the true Catholics and neither could tolerate the other. Both tried to weed out and eliminate people in the opposing camp. Many of us had come all the way to Italy to avoid these battles and to seek a real faith experience.

All I knew about Luigino was in a newspaper article I had read about him a few years before. Now at San Vittorino during that December, 1978, visit I met him: he was a tall, large-boned man with dark eyes, the thinnest lips I have ever seen, and narrow shoulders. He had light-brown splotches on his pink face. It was said that the splotches came in answer to his prayers because he did not want women lusting after him. I couldn't understand why they would: he didn't strike me as handsome at all. He always wore a black cassock or robe, black fingerless gloves, and a cape in cold weather. This costume made an impression of great dignity.

In those days, I was eager to believe, eager to embrace something I could see that could somehow confirm the truth of what I could not see. From the other Americans in residence, I heard stories about Luigino—of miraculous healings, mind-reading, bi-location, exorcisms and of the miraculous scent—the scent of flowers or incense that seemed to emanate from him. It was said that he had the wounds of Christ like St. Francis of Assisi. Since he always wore gloves I could not vouch for that at the time, but I believed it. The scent I did smell, very strongly—it was called the "odor of sanctity."

We soon entered the life of San Vittorino. The seminary itself was a three-story building: a floor for the priests, a floor of dorm rooms for the seminarians and on the bottom floor a cafeteria or refectory, a chapel and a recreation room. A series of bells regulated the day: up at seven, Mass at 7:30, followed by breakfast. On school days the vans would leave for classes in Rome and return by 1:30, after which the afternoon would be devoted to study; then there was "the holy hour," a period of community prayer in the chapel, followed by dinner at eight. This schedule suited me. I had always tried to have a prayer life and go to Mass whenever I could, but here it was all organized for me.

San Vittorino was in a fairly rural area across the freeway from the ancient town of Tivoli. The region was surrounded by fields and distant mountains. The seminary grounds were mostly paved over. I discovered that in many Italian gardens, there was more gravel or cement than greenery. Lawns were considered strictly decorative, never to be walked on. Here and there some shrubs and small trees were growing out of holes in the pavement. I found this strange.

There was construction going on everywhere: a new convent, a large modern church, and a receiving hall for pilgrims. There was a small older chapel, the first building on the property, used for some services. In it there was a statue of the Virgin of Fatima in a glass box. Why is she in a box? I wondered as we prayed in that chapel on some evenings on precarious kneelers which seemed to be on the verge of collapse at any moment.

Since we had arrived toward the end of the semester, most of the Italian seminarians had gone home; only Americans were there. They spent their vacation studying, hiking, and going on day trips organized by the priest in charge, Father Malacelli. Marcus and I decided to live the life of the seminary as much as possible. That would be the best way to make the decision about whether to return as a seminarian.

———

"Mawk!" Chuck called, "get the other Mawk! We're going on a road trip; pack up!" Chuck had adopted us, acting as a big brother during our visit. We were going to Naples and would stop at a church on the way. As we hurried to pack our things I glanced at Marcus. I was excited to be here, but he seemed less enthusiastic, less impressed with the magic of it all. He was much closer to his parents than I was to mine and I thought that he might be struggling with the prospect of moving to Rome.

"Mawks!!!" Chuck shouted.

Riding in the van with about fifteen others, with Chuck on one side incessantly chatting and Marcus on the other silently gazing out the window, I was contented. I finally felt that I was at home; God seemed tangible here. I had seen little of Rome itself, but San Vittorino was enough.

I was thinking of the foreigners we had seen on the seminary grounds in the past few days: during the Christmas season many European groups visited San Vittorino to pray in the tiny chapel while the large modern church was being completed. Everyone who came seemed full of expectations, looking forward to experiencing God and seeing Brother Luigino, *Il Santo*, the saint. I found magic in the Christmas music sung by the German and English choirs who performed during the services. Even though I was very uncomfortable on the hard prehistoric kneelers in that unheated place, I felt safe and supported. I was on the brink of a great adventure; I could feel it. Perhaps this was happiness.

As the van slowed down I became more aware of my surroundings. "What is this place, Chuck?" I asked, as we scrambled out of the van in front of a large church or cathedral.

"I dunno, it has some miraculous picture I think."

"*Nostra Signora della Grazia*," a short, dark-haired Italian priest said.

"Our Lady of Grace." Tony translated; he was a thin seminarian from New York who hadn't said much of anything to me since I arrived. He went on to translate: "The painting is miraculous, since it was painted by Saint Luke and the painting itself floats above the surface of the wall; the paint itself is not attached to anything."

I looked closely at the painting; it was a small, unattractive image, but if it was miraculous, that was enough for me.

I asked Tony, "Has the miracle of the painting been investigated?"

He answered, without consulting the priest-custodian, that scientists had investigated and found that the paint was actually not attached to the wall behind. I wondered how St. Luke had painted that here in Italy. I was amazed at the possibility of the laws of nature being suspended.

"Miraculous painting! And I got to see it!" I told Chuck enthusiastically.

"Yeah, but why are the miraculous paintings always the ugly ones?" he asked, scratching his head.

I laughed, because it was an ugly painting. But I still believed. This was another way to touch the untouchable, another sign I belonged here in this magic place. I was eager to believe and to communicate my belief to others when I returned home.

"*Eccoci*," Father Malacelli announced, as we pulled into the parking lot of a church in Naples. Soon an even shorter priest, with glasses and the typical pasta belly, in a long black robe, was at our van, hugging and kissing Malacelli. As they chatted, I looked around the enclosed parking lot, where groups of twenty or so Neapolitan parishioners were chatting away. I had never seen so many short men in one place at one time.

"Does anyone know what we are doing here?" I asked.

"Eating, I hope," Chuck replied, with a note of desperation. Winter was in the air, the wind was blowing through the bare trees, and the twenty-five of us stood in the parking lot waiting while the two Italian priests chatted and chatted.

"*Bene, andiamo!* Let's go!" Tony urged, after nearly half an hour in the cold.

"*Che bella chiesa!*" Malacelli cried. Tony dryly translated, "What a beautiful church!" as we were led around by this short priest who had not been introduced to us.

"Let's eat," Chuck moaned, while the priest proudly showed us the altars and statues. "*Preghiamo*, let us pray," Tony chirped. Why did I not like him? He seemed stiff, inhuman, almost like a parrot. "Our Father, who art in heaven . . ." I struggled to catch up with the prayers. "Amen."

"And now let's eat!" Tony announced. "*Deo gratias*," Chuck murmured, as we headed to a large hall with long tables set with plates, glasses, bottles and fruit. There were so many plates on the table that there was room for little else. Food came in on platters and kept coming in for the next three hours. Neapolitans value hospitality; sharing food is the sign of friendship. After two hours of continuous consumption, I felt uncomfortably full. Asked again if I wanted a third helping, I said "No, no, no," and tried to wave the server off, but he piled still more food on my plate. The meal was delicious, the hospitality was extreme and I was going to explode.

Notwithstanding my discomfort, everything seemed glorious to me: the drive, the floating fresco, the Neapolitan church, the feast, Chuck's sense of humor. I had discovered a world that I wanted to be part of. I thought Marcus seemed distracted; he laughed and talked, but his mind seemed to be elsewhere. Oh well, I thought to myself, his loss.

The priest had reserved seats for us for a Christmas play that night in a local theatre. None of us Americans could understand a word of the Neapolitan dialect. After about an hour, Chuck nudged me to get up.

"Marcus, come on," I said, but he motioned for me to go on without him.

Chuck led me outside the theatre where there were already five or six Americans smoking and chatting, waiting for the incomprehensible drama to end. After nearly another hour, Malacelli noticed our absence and came to chase us back into our seats. In all, the play lasted four hours. "Why do Italians love to talk so much?" Chuck asked, groaning. At past midnight the play was over; we got into our vans and rode back to Rome too exhausted for conversation.

———

Over the next few days Marcus and I joined in the routine of the seminary: daily prayers, meals, recreation time and several trips to Rome. My life in the U.S. could not compare with what I was discovering here. The stories we were hearing about the resident saint made staying at San Vittorino seem as fascinating as sightseeing in Rome. We were lucky to be able to do both.

"Watch your wallets!" Tim, from Chicago, called as we boarded a No. 64 bus to St. Peter's a few days later. The bus was packed, but we elbowed our way to the upper level to have a better view.

As we pulled up in front of St. Peter's, I asked Tim about an inscription above the basilica. I thought it was probably a passage from the Bible. He said it wasn't; it was a commemoration of the family who wielded great power at the time the basilica was built.

I said I thought it seemed strange that the primary Catholic church in the world had a dedication to a powerful family, and not to Christ.

He said it depended on how you looked at it: there were all sorts of people and events in Church history—saints and sinners, good things and bad. "Why can't God work through all these things, good and bad, to bring about His plan? After all, if it wasn't for these powerful Roman families, maybe St. Peter's would not have been built. Then you wouldn't be here now, would you?"

I began to feel that I too was part of a great history, full of valleys and mountains, greed and sainthood, self-promotion and self-effacement.

When we entered St. Peter's Basilica for the first time, I felt as though I were walking into an emerald city, like Oz. Even the light seemed different: it came down in dramatic shafts, piercing the air. We gazed at the Pietá, walked through the tombs of the popes underneath the floor, explored the side chapels and marveled at the mosaics above the altars.

Time was running out: my two-week visit would be over in a few days. I wanted to come back to San Vittorino in the fall to begin a new life, but I decided that I needed a sign to make sure I was choosing the right path. The seminarians told stories about this Brother Luigino, how he seemed to read hearts, to know what someone had done in private, was going to do, or should do. Several said they were in the seminary because

Brother Luigino had revealed to them that their coming there was God's will. In the last days of our visit this became a fixation for me: I need Luigino to tell me whether I should come back in the fall or whether I should stay in the United States and go on with my old life.

As we walked up a steep path to the large turbine-shaped church for services and Christmas carols, Chuck said, "You guys have become part of us in just a short time; you gotta come back and join us! I'll miss you guys. It's like you're part of the family already."

"I want to," I replied. Night had already fallen. I glanced over at Marcus, who walked with his head down, pensive and withdrawn.

We shivered as we entered the freezing modern church. Even from the inside, it resembled a washing-machine turbine with a central shaft rising above the altar area. Everywhere there were water stains where rain had soaked through the ceiling. Apparently a design defect had caused the structure to crack even during construction. In the center was an altar, on the left a bigger-than-life-size statue of the Madonna of Fatima and on the right, Christ crucified. It was all very worshipful rather than dramatic, but that didn't bother me. Every evening there were prayers and Italian Christmas carols either in the little chapel or the large church, where I noticed that during the Mass the pilgrims gawked at the seminarians as if they were from Pluto.

After the services Chuck stuck with Marcus and me like glue. As Brother Luigino walked across our path, Chuck called out to him: "*Partono domani*—Tomorrow they're leaving!" At that point what seemed to me a miracle occurred: the saint approached us and said: "*Tornate, perche' Iddio vi vuole qua*—Return, because God wants you here." I was stunned: here was my sign! "*Va bene*—okay," was my fumbling reply. Suddenly we found ourselves surrounded, everyone asking us what had been said. "He told us to come back in the fall," I told them. I thought, God has finally revealed my path.

Why is happiness often the expectation of a future illuminated by certainty and hope? Trying to find a valid path, wanting to make my life count, wanting to be part of a great history—these were happiness. Like a lightning flash, I caught a glimpse of my journey.

"Can you believe it? I can't wait to fill out the application form! Can you believe what just happened?!" I bubbled over at Marcus as we walked up to our dorm rooms.

Marcus fired back. "How do you *know* it's the right choice for you, just because Brother Luigino said so? He's not God!"

I was stunned. All these days of silence meant something. Marcus didn't believe! He wasn't convinced! He couldn't see the magic of this place; it was all passing him by. How could he be so blind? Hadn't he seen what I saw, heard what I heard? And he chose not to believe!

"You're lost!" I shot back, as I stomped off to my room. Once alone I relished the revelation and resolved to walk this path without Marcus. It seemed to be the only possibility for happiness for me since every other choice faded into superficiality. It was as if only in this place could I achieve something great.

———

I was back at school in southern California, where Marcus and I were in our first year at Thomas Aquinas, a small liberal arts college. But my heart remained in Italy. "Marcus, look at that plane. I wonder if it might be going to Rome," I said as we walked to our afternoon classes. My daily life at college had become a dream; reality lay in Rome, a world in which faith was not mere doctrine but was filled with tangible signs; it was an adventure to look forward to during the dull daily routine.

"Are you guys going back to Rome to enter the seminary?" Cathy asked as we stood outside the classroom. She was a classmate of ours, a small girl with a short haircut, quick to smile, and when she started laughing she always managed to end up with her whole upper body on a table or desk.

"Yes, in the fall," Marcus replied. He had come around; my longing for that world had started to envelop him. "Mark, do you think we will get to meet the Pope?" he asked.

"I think so; after all, the Pope is very close to Brother Luigino. Maybe he'll even come out to the seminary when we're there!" Cathy was beaming at us.

Thomas Aquinas, where Marcus and I had enrolled after high school, was beautifully set among hills, woods and a large lake. It was a very Catholic environment, with Mass and rosary every day in the college chapel. It was an intellectual and religious environment where I felt comfortable. We had become very popular at the college and our Roman adventure was the talk of the campus for weeks. Everyone wanted to give us advice: most said to stay and complete our degrees before moving to Europe, but I would have none of that. I could barely wait six months to go, let alone three years.

We soon slipped back into a routine of classes, studying, meals, and community prayer. We had begun to attend the evening prayer services on campus. "Come on Marcus, we're going to be late!" I called, irritated that I always had to wait for him . . . The rosary started at seven o'clock in the chapel by the lake, and it was now 6:59. By 7:12 we were kneeling along with a dozen or so students. During the quiet chant of the Hail Mary, my mind often wandered over my life. That evening I began to weep quietly as I often did for some unknown reason during the rosary. I tried to hide it from Cathy, who was kneeling next to me. I cried and cried. I didn't ask myself why I felt this way. I just had a sad feeling that could only be expressed in tears. Perhaps it was because I felt so alone and alienated from everybody; family, friends, companions. Even Marcus couldn't have cared less about my depression. Our friendship was built on common interests and not on common affection. It was a bond with a time limit, an expiration date. I was alone. "Mark,

I want to talk with you after," Cathy whispered. She was on to me, she saw my tears, she would ask, I would have no answer. I made my escape.

—————

In June of 1978 I had successfully completed my first year of college and was back home in Modesto. I had been dreading this inevitable conversation. We were in my bedroom. "Dad, in the fall I'm going to Rome to enter the seminary," I said, bracing myself for his rebukes and irritation. My father was not a bad person, but he had never showed any interest in my life. I knew he wouldn't understand. How could he? Faith for him was a distant memory of the past, wrapped up with my dead mother.

"Why am I the last to know about this?" he asked angrily.

"I wanted to wait to tell you face to face," I said. Actually I had delayed talking to him so that he would have only two months instead of six to tell me what a bad idea it was. I had made my decision when I was still in Rome and I had filled out the application before I left.

"You could have at least discussed it with me before you made your decision. I have a background in education. I have something to say about it . . ." He went on and on; he was irritated and offended, not because I was entering the seminary, but because he was not the first person I had told about it. He made it all about him. He was angry that I was alienated from him, that I had my own sense of direction. Now no matter what he said, I was resolved; I would leave everything behind and never look back with regret. I would embark on the adventure that I had always longed for. All I had to do was to earn 600 dollars for the plane fare. I told my father that I was going to live with my grandmother for the summer. She was alone and needed help.

At age 19, I saw my father as an angry and sometimes even as an evil man. Later I would realize that each person is always a product of his own life, formed by his own experiences and relationships. My father had met my mother in college and they had married after he had enlisted in the Air Force. He began a teaching career when they moved to California. My earliest memories of him are few: he was head of the drama department, and his schedule often kept him busy at school until late. His absence caused an early feeling of alienation from him that persisted when I was a teenager.

Despite the lack of a strong paternal influence, my childhood was by no means unhappy. Growing up in a suburban household with my three siblings was a positive experience, although my mother was frequently ill. I was too young to be aware of how this was affecting my father. To me, he was simply a distant authority figure with no bonds of affection. When my mother was diagnosed with cancer and her health started to fail, my father seemed even more absent; unable to talk with us about what was going on, he buried himself in his work. When my mother died, he fell apart and seemed to have to rely heavily on alcohol to get through his day.

When, a few years after my mother's passing, my father announced that he was planning to remarry, I saw it as a betrayal. This was the perspective of a 15-year-old. In reality, his new relationship lifted him out of his depression and despair and gave him something to look forward to. But I saw a change in him that bothered me: he seemed to become extremely submissive to my new stepmother. Since she was highly educated and somewhat domineering, that may have been the only way their relationship could work.

My father's pain and his attempts to deal with it were not things that I thought about that summer. I had insulated my emotional core against him years before. I didn't want or seek his support. I saw the road now and no one could stop me.

My grandmother, my father's mother, lived a few miles from my parents. I got a job packing fruit, moved into her extra bedroom, and enjoyed staying with her: she was not demanding or confrontational, and she loved to cook. I never heard her say the words "I love you," but she said it through the homemade crepes, stuffed peppers and egg bread often ready for me when I arrived home from work. She was lonely and liked to be active, even if it was only cooking and doing light chores around the house. I was pleased that by staying with her I could keep her company and at the same time avoid dealing with my father.

I soon settled into a routine: I left for work at six a.m., arrived at the pear orchards by seven and packed pears in boxes until late afternoon. It was an outdoor packing plant: the fruit came down a conveyer belt and dropped into a revolving bin, where I packed them, and put the boxes on another conveyer belt to be shipped. My back ached for the first week and every time I closed my eyes I saw revolving pears. But working six days a week I could earn enough for the plane fare to Europe.

The summer months passed like days and soon Marcus and I found ourselves in his parents' car on our way to the airport. That day we realized that our lives were changing; we cried. We were 19 years old and from now on, when we found ourselves back in Modesto, it would only be as visitors. The pain of this departure was acute. But despite my tears, I was extremely excited. I felt as if I were exploring a deep crevice in the ocean that no one had ever seen, or as if I were stepping on a planet for the first time. Life was an adventure and I was about to take part in it.

————

"Marcus," I called back to him, "what do you have in those suitcases? It looks like they're full of bricks!" He struggled behind me as we made our way from the airport to a train in London that would take us to the Channel ferry. This roundabout way saved money.

"Why don't you help?!" he snapped back.

"How? I have my own to lug around!" He could barely walk, his luggage was so heavy. He had filled his suitcases with books that he thought he might need in Rome. I had noticed while we were in college that Marcus had an obsessive streak. One weekend he seemed to be taking forever to pack his suitcase before heading home to Modesto. I asked him impatiently why he was taking so long. Our ride was waiting outside. "I have to make sure that my underwear doesn't touch my Bible—they're both in there together," he said. "I'm trying to keep everything in place when I close it."

I scratched my head and went back to my room to open my suitcase again: my Bible and textbooks were jumbled among my clothes. "Disrespectful or not, I'm not re-packing my suitcase," I mumbled to myself.

Several weeks later I heard loud laughter in the cafeteria; Marcus, surrounded by four female students, was imitating the walk of another student, a senior who was always looking for a husband. He was a clever mimic. I started laughing too; he had her walk down, exaggerating her hip movements. Later in the day he came to my room and asked, "Mark, do you think I should confess that? After all, I was making fun of others."

I shrugged. I really didn't know if it was wrong or right, only that it was funny. But that was Marcus; he was a man divided: spontaneous and guilt-ridden.

Now, on our way back to Rome, we were on a train so crowded that we had to sit on our suitcases in an empty space between two cars. This seemed bearable until the temperature dropped, and for much of the night we were hit by blasts of freezing air every time someone opened the sliding door. And we still needed to cross the English Channel.

"I can't believe this," Marcus groaned as the train doors opened and its passengers poured onto a platform to board a ferry in the middle of the night. Pushing, shoving, running, we still didn't stand a chance to get a seat as we each lugged our three bags at the tail end of the crowd. On the ferry we had to sit on our luggage once more; perhaps we would ride our suit-cases all the way to Rome.

So far this journey was horrible: I had left California in tears, arrived in London emotionally exhausted, and on this ferry we were both uncomfortable, cold, and tired. But I felt excited; all of this discomfort was secondary, like a mediocre preface to a great novel. A sense of expectation and joy filled me that cold night bobbing on the Channel; what was begin-ning to unfold would be greater than anything I had ever expe-rienced. I was certain of that and this certainty made every difficulty bearable.

"Hurry up, Marcus, lets get a seat this time! I'll go ahead!" I shouted as I ran and pushed my way off the ferry to board the awaiting train. To my delight we found two open seats in a compartment. We settled back and watched the landscape whiz by, mostly green hills and old buildings. When we crossed the border into Italy many more people boarded the train, to the point that there were no more seats. I noticed an Italian couple sitting on two pull-out stools in the corridor in front of our compartment. They caught my attention because the man was holding a newspaper on both their laps and from the position of his arm it was clear that he was reaching up her skirt. And she seemed to have her hand inside his pants. I was shocked. I had never seen such a thing in public. I was new to Italy and her mysterious ways.

Arriving in Rome on a hot August day in 1978, we stag-gered across the Stazione Termini towards the bus stop for San Vittorino. We hadn't slept in days, had eaten very little for lack of money, and I still hoped that the little scratch I felt in my throat was just from fatigue. I was in Rome, the place of my dreams! But I was too tired to think about it. We boarded the bus and, after about an hour, found ourselves dragging our luggage towards the seminary.

Our arrival was a blur. We were given rooms and I immedi-ately went to bed without eating. I was so sick the next morning that I couldn't leave my room. I was in bed for ten days. Marcus didn't come around much; he was exploring this new world, the new faces and wonders. I, in the meantime, was trying to figure out what this large wax rocket-shaped pill was that the Italian seminarian gave me when he found out I had a fever. Somehow it didn't seem as though I could swallow it, but I couldn't imagine what I was supposed to do with it. So I put it in my drawer.

"Marco, *ti senti di venire giu*—do you feel like coming downstairs?" Maurizio asked me. He had been appointed nurse because he had been a medical student. He was medium height, with acne and glasses. I would come to find out that he played a significant role in seminary life. But for now the only thing I noticed was that he stood too close to me when he talked. When I stepped back he stepped forward, as if he could not digest my words unless his nose was four inches from mine.

"*Si, per la cena*—yes, for dinner," I replied.

The refectory was filled with long tables holding wooden bowls of fruit—apples and pears—and bottles of wine and bottled water. The priests sat separately at a table in the middle of the large room; at the side tables were about sixty seminarians, half of them Italian, with a sprinkling of French Canadians and Africans, and the rest *Americani*. For some reason, the Italian seminarians' clothes were always gray or navy blue—was there a dress code that no one had told us about? Everyone stood behind his chair as the priest in charge, Father Malacelli, led the Italian prayer.

Cena—dinner—was a watery soup with tiny bits of pasta, bread, a slice of luncheon meat, fruit, and bottles of a yellow sour liquid that someone said was wine. I spied gnats floating in some of the bottles on our table. I didn't understand the food or the clothes or much of the language, but my spirits were high. I was in Rome to begin this great adventure. I would be able to see things that few have seen and experience things few would experience. "Mark, try this to make your soup better," Charles, a seminarian sitting next to me said, as he tore bread up and dropped it in his soup, making a hot flavorful mush that I came to enjoy.

Recreazine—recreation would become a daily ritual for the next five years. After lunch and dinner, an obligatory time was set aside for us to gather outside to talk, get to know one another, occasionally play sports, or take long walks. It was sort of a forced "get to know one another session," but I liked it. The story of how each of us had arrived in that place was fascinating to me and I could practice my fledging attempts at Italian. However, when Brother Luigino, *Il Santo*, came out to join us, the focus changed. Most of the Italians stopped whatever they had been doing, and gathered around him, encircling him as he strolled, like a walking football huddle. I felt torn: should I go with Brother Luigino and try to understand what he was saying, or stay and enjoy chatting with the other Americans? It was a daily choice, and most of the time I chose *Il Santo*.

———

It was a warm September afternoon and, as usual after lunch, a group was gathered around Brother Luigino, hanging onto his every word. Maurizio was writing down what Luigino said in a notebook; I never understood why he did it, he recorded all Luigino's words the entire time I was in that seminary.

Over the past several weeks Brother Luigino never seemed to pay any attention to me; it was as if I was made of glass and he was looking through me at whomever was behind me. I longed for recognition, for validation from a man believed to be so close to God. I wanted to know from him that I was in good standing, or at least on the right path. Since I was often in Luigino's line of vision, listening to his words about faith and life, why didn't he see me?

I was seeking affirmation in those days. I seemed to need my value and worth to be confirmed by others before I could be convinced of it myself. Since Brother Luigino was so close to

God, his validation would be a divine seal. I didn't know how to love myself; only if another loved me, one who was close to God, would I be convinced that I could be loved by others as well as by the Divine.

And then suddenly one day I was no longer invisible.

"*Vieni con me*—come with me," Brother Luigino said when the other seminarians were preparing to return to their rooms at the end of recreation time. I followed him, a huge black figure in his long robe, back into the room where he met pilgrims who came from all over Italy seeking his prayers and advice. Excited that I was finally recognized, I felt great anticipation as I prepared to share my heart with the *Santo*. He brought me to his small receiving room; divided in half by a grill, it looked like a jail cell. He sat behind the grill; I was told it had been put there to prevent fanatical visitors from grabbing him or seizing parts of his clothing as relics. I sat on the other side of the grill, but he beckoned to me. "*Vieni qua*—come over here."

I went to him. My Italian was poor then, but he made it clear to me that I was indeed recognized. He embraced me, and asked, "*Mi vuoi bene?*—Do you love me?" I knew that this question was merely an expression of innocent affection. He embraced me and I stood and received the embrace. Even though I was emotionally excited and somewhat aroused, it was a hug that could not be motivated by sensuality because *Il Santo* would never act out of sexual desire. He made the sign of the cross on my heart and said "*Addesso questo e' mio*—now this heart is mine." Then he asked me to pull up my shirt, made the sign of the cross on my chest and before I could pull my shirt down, held me again, pressing my bare chest against his, heart to heart. He repeated, "*Tuo cuore e' mio cuore*—your heart is my heart." I felt happy, safe and, finally, loved.

Going back to my room, I believed I had a particular rapport with Brother Luigino that no one else could share in or know. My arousal during the encounter, I thought, was due to my own lack of progress in the spiritual life. Brother Luigino loved me, the *Santo* loved me; what a great sign to rejoice in! This was God loving me through him.

The next day, as I participated in the daily huddle around Brother Luigino, along with the Italians and a few Americans, I expected that now I would have a closer relationship with him. Our private meeting had been a giant leap: he had seen into my heart and had not been disappointed; he still loved me. My feeling of unworthiness caused by my sexual stirrings, as well as my lack of self-confidence, was overcome by the encounter. I was glowing from the experience; could this be the glow of holiness that the saints write about?

But on that day, as well as on the days that followed, I was still the transparent man, as if our encounter had never happened. Why? I thought that Brother Luigino must know best— after all, he was a saint. He probably didn't want me to become too attached to him. His ignoring me must be a good thing, I thought.

Soon it became clear that Maurizio was closest to Luigino. All of Luigino's conversation was directed to Maurizio, while a dozen or so others always gathered around trying to catch a glance or a word. Maurizio had special privileges: he could stay up later than the rest of us, be absent from recreation time, and go to the priest's floor, which was forbidden to us. Maurizio continued to busily scribble down every word that left Luigino's lips as if he was transcribing God's words.

I missed Chuck and the others who had welcomed us to the seminary the previous December. They had moved on to another house to begin their Novitiate, the second stage of their seminary formation. At San Vittorino, I had to create my own family and sense of belonging; sometimes following Brother Luigino around all day made this difficult. I was actually pleased when one day he didn't come out to recreation because he had another engagement. Maurizio came outside and I watched him as I chatted with Amadeo, an Italian seminarian. Maurizio wandered from person to person; he didn't seem to have any rapport with anyone, probably because he had been with only Luigino since our arrival in the seminary several weeks earlier. I resolved not to allow that to happen to me.

"*Da dove sei*—where are you from?" Amadeo asked. He was of medium height by Italian standards, had a round face and prominent ears, but his most noticeable feature was his voice: the most high-pitched that I had ever heard from man or woman. I tried to ignore it, as if I was chatting with a man with two noses while trying not to stare. He was from Belluno, high in the Dolomites, a place I was later to visit.

I asked him why he had come to the seminary. He told me about his promise to God, about entering the seminary if his then-bishop from Belluno was made pope. That did happen: the bishop became John Paul I. Amadeo struck me as relatively uneducated but intelligent, with a sense of humor. It was his sense of humor that drew me to him. I resolved to get to know Amadeo better, to practice my Italian on him and to develop our friendship.

———

"Mark, how's it going?" It seemed the question of a stranger. I hadn't really exchanged two words with Marcus since our arrival. In high school we had had much in common, because we were the only ones there who were interested in the Church. But here, with about sixty men in the seminary for the same purpose, Marcus and I suddenly had nothing in common at all. What had seemed to be a close friendship faded into the misty Roman night. I saw him spending time with other Americans as well as Italians, and I asked myself what had been missing from our friendship. I realized that Marcus had no real feeling for me. He came from a close-knit family; he was his mother's pride and joy and it always seemed to me that she treated him as if he were still ten years old. He was accustomed to being the center of attention and affection—a far cry from my experience with my own family.

——

The pontifical universities open on October 15 each year. After six weeks of Italian language classes and time spent at the seminary, we began the daily trek into Rome to the University of St. Thomas, or Angelicum University, where we embarked on the courses of philosophy necessary for the bachelors degree. I had studied some classical philosophy and wanted to learn more. However, I found that most of the seminarians, both Italian and American, viewed the philosophy courses as superfluous, and considered only theology to be of value. Americans did the least work necessary to pass the classes, with no real interest in learning the material. The Italians tended to get through their courses by crash studying at the end of the semester and cheating on the exams.

I had heard that the Italians not only cheated but justified that as perfectly ethical. I saw some people bringing answer sheets into the tests. In fact, most exams at the Angelicum were now oral, because cheating had disabled the entire examination system. Heated arguments at San Vittorino had reached the point where there was a division in the seminary between Americans and Italians. Was it right to cheat on an exam? For weeks there were arguments and tempers flared, as people said things they would regret. One day I shouted at an Italian, "That's why, when you go to an Italian hospital for appendicitis, they amputate your leg! All the Italian doctors cheated themselves through medical school!"

Tension was high. It was our introduction to another culture and a mentality very different from our own. It seemed self-evident to the Americans that cheating on an exam was not a good thing and certainly not morally defensible. Why couldn't the Italians see what was so obvious? But they refused to accept our position. Finally, to resolve the question, it was decided to bring it to Brother Luigino: since he was so close to God, he would surely see the truth of the matter.

Maurizio was the spokesperson. About fifteen seminarians gathered around to hear the verdict: "Is it immoral to cheat or to help someone by cheating on an exam?" he asked.

"Puo' essere anche un atto di carita' auitare un'altro durante un'esame—it can certainly be an act of charity to help someone else during an exam." That was Luigino's answer.

The verdict was in and the Americans were wrong. Cheating is not unethical. We were dumbfounded. "Brother Luigino, being a saint, is still Italian in his thinking," one American commented as we walked away, disillusioned.

The library at the Angelicum was unlike an American library in that none of the books was accessible. I pleaded with the librarian, "I need to find the commentary on Thomas Aquinas that my professor recommended."

"Fill this out," he said, pushing a form toward me.

"Can I go browse, and get it for myself?"

"No, no, no! This library doesn't function like that."

"Well, okay, but I'd like to check the book out. Can I have it for three weeks?"

"You cannot check out books. You can only read the book here in the room. If I let students check out books we would lose them all."

"But this book is required reading. Can't you set it out for us to use?"

"Three times I set it out and three times it was stolen by the Italians. No, I cannot put it out."

What is this, I thought to myself? How can one be a seminarian and steal books from a pontifical university and not see anything wrong with it? Why can't they see the contradiction in this? I was an American and I was baffled.

Traditional European teaching was through lectures, usually in a large room or *aula*. The professor might supply the

students with outlines, but as a rule he did not. He lectured for
the entire period while the students took notes. At the end of
the semester there would be a ten-minute oral exam to determine one's grade. I felt what can only be described as panic,
as I sat in class not understanding a word of the Italian lecture
spoken, falling behind in my studies day by day without being
able to do a thing about it.

"Don't worry," one of the seminarians reassured me. "Theology is the only thing that matters anyway."

I knew better. Philosophy had given me a rational base that
I valued: the ability to reason, to use logic, to think critically,
to separate fact from fiction and emotion. I wanted to delve
more deeply into Plato and Aristotle, but I was lost here.

Browsing through the library at San Vittorino, I found only
a few philosophy texts. The shelves were filled with devotional
works: biographies of saints, especially St. Therese; intro-
ductions to the spiritual life; treatises on prayer. In one stack
of books I found *The Divine Comedy* and several historical
philosophy texts, as well as one on metaphysics. I took them,
resolving to read them and learn something until my Italian
improved. I also decided to re-read Aristotle, especially the sections on logic and metaphysics. This plan calmed me down
somewhat.

Searching for books, I came across another closet in the
library I had never noticed before. Opening it, I was surprised
to find it filled with very odd objects: Hallowe'en supplies,
cups, party favors, and ten or twelve stuffed animals. There
was a hawk with full wing-spread, an armadillo, a duck, and
several smaller creatures. My panic over school faded as I tried
to think of ways I could use these to lighten the solemn atmosphere of the seminary.

I read the philosophical texts I took from the library fer-
vently, taking notes. They covered only a little of the same content as the class. I read Dante for pleasure, and finding myself

drawn into his world of hope, happiness, and consequences. I put the book down and thought about the hidden closet, about what I could do with those stuffed animals, who would take the joke good-naturedly.

There was a knock on my door, and Sean came in; he was an Irish seminarian with a PhD, a year ahead of me. "Don't worry about the exams," he said. "I'm going to make copies of all my outlines from last year and pass them around for you guys to study from. I have everything you need to know."

"Great! Thanks, Sean," I said, "that's a big relief."

With my worries assuaged, my thoughts returned to the mysterious closet and I started to plan my first practical joke. "Amadeo," I called after dinner, "let's talk."

Amadeo and I had a long conversation on the patio that night about his family in Belluno and my life in California. Suddenly I noticed it was late; at ten o'clock the bell would ring and then there was the Grand Silence; we were not allowed to speak until the next morning at breakfast. After prayers we went to our rooms.

I heard nothing until the next morning. But at breakfast everyone was laughing and talking about what Amadeo had found when he went upstairs to bed. "That was funny, Mark," Francis from Chicago said. "I liked the armadillo in his bed instead of his pillow. But the best one was the hawk with the wings spread over his whole room."

Amadeo wagged his finger at me. "I'll get you, you will see," he said, laughing. I had placed ten stuffed animals in his small cubicle that night. "I had to stay up until eleven just to bring them back to the library!" he said. Everybody enjoyed that prank, but what I didn't realize was that I had unleashed an onslaught of practical jokes that would come full circle.

I fell into a routine: rising at 6:30 in the morning and lights out at 10:30 at night. I found a certain comfort in this; a sense of stability and direction where there had been mostly confusion. The seminary rules were strict and the rector, Fr. Malacelli, had a quick temper. Although he had a good heart, he mostly inspired fear. I tried to keep out of his way.

My cubicle was the last at the end of the corridor. One night I looked out the window and was surprised by the starry night; the Roman city lights could not be seen in San Vittorino so hundreds of stars were clearly visible. It became a ritual for me to look at the night sky from that window before I went to bed. To the ancient Greeks the stars were eternal, unchanging, and that immutability became a consolation for me. No matter what happened, the stars would lift my spirits and remind me of those things that do not change. I began to long for something beyond the daily life in the seminary. I didn't understand that longing, I couldn't even express it, but it began in that first year.

The intense atmosphere of the seminary, coupled with the load of studies in a foreign language, created a certain tension from which people wanted an outlet. Word had gotten around that I had played a practical joke, so it was only a matter of time before I became a victim. It was much more entertaining being the perpetrator, I thought to myself one night when I returned to my room after the Grand Silence had begun, to find that both my door and my bed were gone. Fortunately I was able to track them down by following the trail of muffled laughter in the next corridor.

The Italians, encouraged to learn English, were required on certain days to speak English at dinner. Most of them knew only a few words. Amadeo sat across from me and his English vocabulary was particularly limited. He struggled to find the words to ask the person next to him to pass the soup. He asked Steve, sitting on his other side, to tell him how to say that in English

"Pass the soup," he repeated after Steve, and asked, "*Come si dice 'per favore,'* how does one say 'please' in English?"

Paul told him that the English word for "*per favore*" is "dog face." So Amadeo turned to the person next to him and said in perfect English: "Pass the soup, dog face."

There was a shocked silence, then everyone burst into laughter. Amadeo was perplexed at first, but before he left the table after dinner, he told Steve he would pay him back for that.

I had fewer courses than the other seminarians because I had taken several philosophy classes in college and I used those free hours to explore Rome near the Angelicum. During the school day, I visited the Forum; St. Peter's in Chains and its Moses; St. Mary Major and its relics of Christ's crib, and the Coliseum. Fr. Malacelli strictly forbade us to go into Rome for sightseeing; we were allowed to take the van in once a week, only if we needed to buy personal items. I found a way to see some Roman sights without directly violating his rule. I always went on my own. I wanted to explore, to see, to know, to discover as much as I could.

Fr. Malacelli's policies were baffling. He forbade us to go to Rome to sightsee, although the Vatican was there. He would not allow a Christmas tree in the seminary, saying it was a pagan symbol, yet even the Pope had one set up in St. Peter's Square. Our mail had to pass through Malacelli's hands. He explained this rule one day during a conference. "In my time the mail was read by the superior and censored before being handed out. I retain the right to do so even though I will probably not use that right. I will distribute the mail as it arrives."

Once when he was away, our mail sat upstairs for four days until he got back. Letters from home had become precious to us Americans; they were like an oasis in a desert. On the third day I could stand it no longer; I went upstairs with two other seminarians to look for our letters in the pile of mail. I didn't find anything, but what I had done was reported to Malacelli: he reprimanded me for it in public during the next conference. I felt shame, regret and hurt, but I didn't see why he should control our mail. Sometimes I respected Malacelli, but at other times I detested him.

Among his other talents, Brother Luigino was an artist. The seminary was filled with his paintings: Stations of the Cross, one of Christ, hanging above the chapel door and a dozen or so others, always religious subjects, throughout the seminary. Luigino said that he painted late at night and his hand was guided by God's Spirit. This made his artwork extremely valuable in the eyes of the seminarians and visitors to the shrine.

Hundreds of visitors came to San Vittorino every week to see the "Saint," to ask for his prayers, and to tour the shrine. Busses would pull up and spill the pilgrims onto the asphalt in front of the shrine. They were mostly groups of Italians, and the majority were women, middleaged or older. Once in a while foreigners would come; I was always curious to see them. After the visitors' prayer service or Mass, they would meet *Il Santo* who gave a holy card to each pilgrim. To a few he granted the honor of speaking with him privately in the small caged room where I had been. Why would so many come? He was said to be a saint; to have the wounds of Christ, so for many he was a way to find God. They came, too, to see his religious paintings.

Brother Luigino's artistic style was distinctive: the hands on his figures were block-like and sometimes disproportionate or anatomically impossible. I wasn't sure how to reconcile this with the claim that God was painting through him. No one dared to criticize his work; in fact, everyone marveled at all of it.

Myles, who was from Michigan and one year ahead of me, had a quick wit. As we walked into the chapel for night prayers one evening, he pointed up at Luigino's portrait of a disproportionate Christ, and remarked, "He *must* be God, to be able to hold his hand in that position." I chuckled through the evening prayers.

After the first three or four months of seminary life, there were rumors that several Americans were considering leaving, having apparently decided that this was not their calling. The topic came up during one of the daily gatherings around Brother Luigino. Sitting under some olive trees, he said to one of those Americans, "God can do anything; if it were not His will that you be here He would have put any number of obstacles in front of you to prevent you from arriving. He could have made the airplane not take off, the train not arrive, or any number of things. But He didn't prevent you from coming—on the contrary. Therefore, it is His will that you stay. Any other thoughts come from the Evil One and are only a temptation to abandon His will for you."

The seminarian in question left anyway. But when I returned to my room that day, I reflected on Luigino's words. He seemed to be saying that God acts through events in one's life, and so one's own feelings are unreliable. Since you are here in the seminary, it is God's will that you be here and that you stay here. For years after that day I tried to live my life according to these words. I am here in the seminary and it is God's will that I stay and walk this road. If I feel sad or empty, I should ignore these feelings for they mean nothing. They are like the wind, leading nowhere.

To ignore my feelings I had to rely on my will, so I resolved to strengthen my will by following my mind rather than my heart. After all, I thought, weren't we taught to follow the spirit rather than the flesh? My emotions were influenced by changing conditions like fatigue or rest, need or fulfillment, sexuality or self-denial. These might change every day. I had to follow what I *knew* and not what I *felt*. This was the road I must take because *Il Santo* said it was the right road.

The seminary rooftop, accessible through a small door, became one of my favorite sanctuaries if I had a few moments to myself. From there, across the freeway, the beautiful ancient city of Tivoli was plainly visible, hugging the hillside. It looked so small from where I stood. There was Hadrian's Villa; a vast palace and gardens built for the emperor, his wife and his lover Antinous. On the other horizon were bluish mountains and olive groves. But my favorite view was a distant patch of green field or meadow. That place would become my focus; in my two years at San Vittorino the longing born from the stars

would settle on that meadow and I would yearn to be there,
to transport myself there, to wander and live in that field, far
from my daily routine. Was this an expression of unhappiness?
I didn't think so at the time. After all, these were mere feelings,
not to be trusted. Later I would come to see that longings like
that are often signs of a deep restlessness and discontent. Many
years had to pass before that became clear to me.

"Amadeo, what will you do over vacation?" I asked one evening in November. The Italians were starting to make Christmas plans; the Americans stayed in Italy for the three-week
winter break.

"Help my mother and my priest," he replied in his shrill
voice.

I enjoyed Amadeo's company and thought of him as a
friend. He was fun, easy to talk with and intelligent in a commonsense sort of way. One day he told me that he actually
had two voices: the one he used in everyday conversation and
a low voice that sounded like an earthquake. It seems that, in
puberty, instead of his voice cracking and eventually changing, he retained the high voice of his childhood and developed
a parallel, lower voice. But the higher voice was too high and
the lower voice was too low. So he chose to use the higher one.
When I persuaded him to demonstrate his lower voice to me,
my jaw dropped. It was the voice of a underground ogre who
shook the boulders above him when he spoke. I tried not to
show how amazed, and even unnerved, I was.

During Christmas vacation there was more time to catch
up on studies as well as to get to know the other American
and Canadian seminarians. Several excursions were planned
to nearby sites: Hadrian's Villa across the freeway, and Orvi-
eto and Viterbo, medieval towns with beautiful churches and
art. Holidays were a time too when many became homesick; it
seemed as though every five minutes a call was coming in from

America for one of them.

On the terrace one evening, Yves from Quebec commented that I never got calls from home. He asked, "Why don't you ever talk about your family?" It was true; I never spoke about my family. I was embarrassed that I received no calls from home during the holidays. I didn't expect any. I never got any letters from home asking about life in the seminary. Was I enjoying it? What was I up to?

Perhaps my family was intimidated by my piety. Maybe they didn't know how to relate to me—religious and secular people often find nothing in common. This had always been the case in my family, especially since my mother's death. But that first Christmas away from home, I had to think that they didn't care about me, about my interests and my new life. And I didn't want anyone in the seminary to know that my mother was dead. My family's apparent indifference and my mother's death were still open wounds. "I don't know," I told Yves. I shrugged and changed the subject.

Most American and Canadian seminarians came from devout Catholic families. Americans tended to come to San Vittorino seeking a "good seminary"; Canadians, because a priest in Montreal had influenced them to come. There were also several Nigerians at San Vittorino: one, Livinus, was naturally good-natured and friendly, with a refreshing simplicity.

One morning Livinus asked me what cornflakes were. After I explained that Americans eat them for breakfast and that they are delicious with a little sugar, I got up to fetch some jam. When I returned to the table, to my horror I found that he had poured hot tea over the cornflakes and was eating them.

"Livinus!" I cried. "No! Eat them with milk!"

"That's okay," he said, laughing. "They're good like this too." Next time, he said, he would try them with milk.

During our day trips Livinus found it an adventure to see and touch snow for the first time. He was a joy to be with because he was always ready to smile. He possessed a gentle spirit that I learned to value and to love.

When the Italians returned from their vacation, it was time for the final exams of the first term. Sean had given out his outlines for the courses that our group was to be tested on, but his material proved to be useless. It was so condensed that it was incomprehensible unless one had already grasped the content of the class. Sean reassured me: "Don't worry about it; just talk as long as you can and keep repeating the same points and the same key words. Their English isn't very good anyway; you'll do fine." I hoped he was right.

I rode to school that day studying Sean's outlines. The van pulled up the hill into the Angelicum parking lot. The university was in an old convent building to which classrooms had been added. Atop the building was a baroque chapel filled with marble and gilding. It had a cold feeling. The classrooms were built around a small central garden and fountain; each room for the philosophy courses had about 200 seats, much like American lecture halls. There were windows on one side, a podium and desk up front and a creaky wooden door. The university was run by the Dominicans, an order infused with the theology of Thomas Aquinas. Since Aquinas used the Aristotelian system in his theology, our philosophy courses dealt primarily with the writings of Aristotle and Plato.

Stopping at the front gate, I took a deep breath. I wanted the next few hours to flash past; I was convinced I would fail all my exams. While we waited outside the examination room, after having signed up on the list posted on the door, I was hoping that right before my first exam I would have a heart attack or be struck by lightning. I was convinced that sudden death would be more merciful than what was about to take place between the professor and me in the ten-minute session.

Once in the room, I sat down and followed Sean's advice, speaking as long as possible, repeating key words and phrases. "*Bene*," the professor said, "good." I did indeed pass exam after exam without really knowing much about the material.

When it was all over I was of course pleased that I had passed, but depressed that I had learned so little.

By February, a few months into the second term, I found myself getting a much better grasp of Italian. It was as if my ear had suddenly adjusted to the sounds and I was able to follow along in class and even to take notes. But there was one professor of metaphysics whom everyone said was brilliant and holy, who gave his lectures and published his material in Latin. I was completely lost in his classes, but remained confident that I could pass the oral exam by using my usual method. My stress lessened and I settled into a more productive study routine.

As the weeks rolled by at San Vittorino, I felt both contented and distressed. I was not mature enough to understand what I was going through, and I didn't trust my emotions. I began to have stomach pains in the evenings. These became so strong that I could hardly stand. Once I got into bed the pain would ease and was always gone by the next morning. I sought refuge in reading and in gazing out the window at the stars. This went on for several years.

When one feels pain in one's arm, it is the body signaling that one should pay attention to that part of the body. It is the same with emotional issues; if one feels sad or upset, nature is signaling one to investigate, to find the cause and a cure. If one ignores these emotional signals, bodily discomfort follows. We often ignore these signals because we don't want to face the gravity of a problem. If one is in a relationship that is not working out, often feelings are suppressed as a form of denial. Human instinct is always more perceptive than intellect. Much suffering could be avoided if one could tune one's mind to one's heart. But I had no idea how to do that.

As winter progressed, the seminary grew cold; the heat was turned on for only four hours a day: two hours in the morning while we were at school and two hours in the evening. Since our rooms were actually cubicles with six-foot walls, it was impossible to build up any warmth within one's space. One evening I was so cold that I was wrapped in my blanket, studying at my desk and warming my hands under my desk lamp. Suddenly I heard a fluttering above my head. I looked up and saw a bat whirling in circles above my cubicle.

Startled, I dashed out into the corridor. Everyone was trying to catch the bat, throwing shoes, shirts, towels at it. There was bedlam. An Italian seminarian got a broom and swung it with all his might, only to hit John from Michigan over the head. When that happened, I crept back into my room for my own safety, letting the others fight it out. After another hour of commotion there was silence; apparently the bat was gone.

———

Seminary life tended to revolve around the liturgical year, especially Christmas and Easter. Some months into the second term, Lent began on Ash Wednesday. It seemed a dreary season as the period of penance began. Winter rains in Rome bring grayness: the sky is gray, the buildings are gray, even the people look gray. Lent compounded this grayness; it seemed to be a season of sacrifice and bad weather. But it was meant to be a spiritual time, and we were encouraged to go to confession every week, especially during Lent.

The confessor was a white-haired Canadian priest named Fr. Brough. He had a red, round, jolly face, and his clothes never fit. I wanted to take my formation seriously, so I began to go to him weekly. But no matter what I said to him, he merely repeated the sermon he had given the Sunday before.

"Father Brough," I finally said to him, "I've been going to confession every week now, but I really don't know what to confess. On a normal day I go to school, come home and eat lunch, study, go to holy hour, eat, then go to bed. Weeks can go by like that. What am I supposed to be confessing here, since I really don't do anything other than that?" I felt upset, thinking that something was wrong with me: I must be sinning and not know it.

"You're looking for the big things only. Look for the smaller things. In last Sunday's readings . . ." he droned on. I decided I would confess things I really didn't think were wrong; maybe things like, "I wasn't kind enough, I wasn't attentive enough." I thought that maybe that was what I was supposed to say. I resolved to keep going to confession weekly and to try to live the spirit of the season as best as I could.

Word got around that Brother Luigino showed his stigmata during Lent, and only the seminarians were permitted to see his pierced hands. I certainly wanted to see this miraculous phenomenon with my own eyes, so I stayed especially close to him during that time. Everyone wanted to see those wounds that drew pilgrims from far and wide. Weeks went by and there was no sign that he was going to reveal anything. Some gave up and stopped following him around all the time. I was tempted to give up too.

One afternoon, however, when most of the others had gone off to study, I did witness the unveiling. He removed his black fingerless gloves, and revealed white gauze wrapped around each wrist. He unwrapped it and then showed his hands; the wounds were actually in his wrists, not his palms. The holes did not appear to go all the way through even though they were on both sides. Each wound looked like the skin pulled back, in a square shape on the front and back of each wrist, revealing red tissue. I had thought that the wounds would go all the way through as they did with St. Francis of Assisi. In any case, I was grateful that I was one of the witnesses; those who missed it were quite upset.

Hundreds of pilgrims came to San Vittorino hoping for a glimpse of the wounds or just to meet *Il Santo*. At times I found the curiosity of the visitors strange; they stared at Luigino as if at any moment they would see a miracle. I wanted to see his wounds because I had heard so much about them and I felt that if I saw them, I would be part of a special, chosen group.

I felt the need to be "special" more than a need for some sort of confirmation of Luigino's sanctity. Many came to the shrine out of a need to witness a sign as confirmation of their faith. In a way that seemed reasonable, for how can one believe in what one cannot see unless one can see something? Faith, for me too, had never been a leap into darkness, but a glimpse of something greater than my capacity to understand. For me to trust in faith I must have that glimpse, I must experience something. But this sign did not have to be a miracle. It just had to be evidence; my faith had to be reasonable.

At times it seemed to me that the visitors marveled at Luigino, focused on him, without letting the experience lead them to God. It was as if they were driving on a freeway and saw a man holding a red sign saying "Right turn next exit." Instead of turning right they stopped, got out of their car, walked over to the man and said, "It's good of you to stand out here. What a great thing you are doing for us on the road. What a beautiful place this is! And you are such a nice person. We will stay with you here instead of going on; you, this place, is enough for us."

———

"What are you guys talking about?" Larry asked three of us who were standing in a circle chatting and joking one night after dinner. One of us told him that we were joking about how I had started laughing yesterday during the night prayer and made other people laugh too, till the whole chapel was out of control. It was true; Myles had made me laugh again last night just before we entered the chapel.

Larry scolded us. "You shouldn't joke about prayer." He was from Michigan, tall, long-faced, blond, and always smiling. He saw his role as correcting his "brothers" when they erred or were uncharitable. When Larry came into a room all joviality would cease. After this happened a few times I dubbed him

Killjoy, a name that stuck with him for many years. I didn't like him because he didn't seem human, he never seemed to let down his guard, never relaxed but was always poised to do the "right thing" and make others do the "right thing." Where was the real Larry behind all the piety and rules?

I hadn't spoken to Marcus in ages, but I asked him what he thought about being corrected all the time by Larry. "He is a kill joy," Marcus said. "I'm going to tell him that he's not the conscience of the community."

I noticed that Marcus's fun side seemed to be predominant lately. But his scrupulous half was never far behind. Just as he did in college, whenever he let off steam, he felt guilty and depressed. Once, for example, a group of us were out in the front yard at night and Marcus, who always sat in the back of the chapel during prayers because he played the organ, began to imitate different men. He parodied the walking and genuflecting style of about a dozen people; it was really funny. The next day he came to me and said, "I feel bad about last night. Do you think I was uncharitable?"

I often wished that he would just stick to being the fun Marcus. But he feared that part of himself. He had been undisciplined in high school and believed that he needed to suppress that part of his personality to prevent it from taking over. This fear would eventually make him intolerant of other people; without self-acceptance he could not accept anyone else.

"Penny for your thoughts," Larry said to me in the van on the way to school one morning. I didn't think anyone really used that expression. "Just daydreaming," I said curtly.

"About what?" He pressed on. Did he have no social skills?

I felt invaded, so I put up my wall: "Nothing in particular."

Actually, I had been thinking about my encounter with Brother Luigino months before. The warmth from that meeting had faded, and now I longed for the attention and affection of the saint. I wanted more confirmation that I was, somehow, special. I decided that I would request another meeting with him to get advice and affirmation. It was usually some weeks after that request was made that one was called to a meeting with him. But I didn't mind waiting.

"We're here, everybody!" Larry cried when the van stopped in front of the university. I told myself that I should try not to judge him so harshly.

Holy Week soon arrived, school was out on holiday and the atmosphere in the seminary grew more intense. The week began with a three-day retreat given by a Dominican, Father Vanstenkiste. He was stooped and white-haired, with a long pink face and thick black-rimmed glasses. He always wore his white Dominican habit with matching white socks. He was the professor from the Angelicum whose notes were published only in Latin. At school I used to wonder if he were aware at all that the classroom was filled with 200 students, none of whom knew one word of Latin. People said he was a holy man, so he was invited to give us the conferences. The retreat consisted of two talks each day, prayer and silence. During the times set aside for meditation I often found myself asleep in bed: I was exhausted from the months of commuting to Rome, learning Italian, studying philosophy and living in the seminary. I decided not to feel guilty about it.

Everyone seemed impressed by the retreat conferences, but I thought they were more suited to the classroom than to an atmosphere of meditation. The professor began with "The virtues according to Saint Thomas," and his presentations remained on an elevated intellectual level. I was relieved when, three days later, the retreat concluded. When we came down to breakfast that next morning there was a new exuberance in the air, a sense of relief that those intense days of silence were over and a delight in being able to talk and enjoy one another's company again.

I noticed that in Rome the weather seemed often to echo the liturgical mood or season. Perhaps it was my imagination, but important feast days seemed always to be clear and sunny, while periods of penance like Advent or Lent were overcast and stormy. When the retreat began on Monday, right on schedule, the stormy weather moved in. By Holy Thursday the clouds had burned away and it was gloriously sunny and warm. The grayness of Lent was gone as the joy of Easter approached.

I was very much looking forward to the Tridium: Holy Thursday, Good Friday and Easter Sunday. It had always been a spiritually and emotionally intense three days for me. I was curious, too, about what was going to happen with Brother Luigino. "Every year, beginning on Holy Thursday," Tim from Illinois told a group of us after lunch, "Brother Luigino undergoes the passion with Christ. He goes through everything that Christ did: the agony in the garden, the trial before Pilate, the flogging and crowning with thorns and finally the crucifixion, when he actually dies—his heart stops beating—for several minutes."

Someone asked, "How do you know that happens?"

Tim said there was always a team of doctors there when it was going on, and that on Good Friday, usually in the morning, all the seminarians would be able to go to the saint's room for a minute or two to witness his passion. "It's a spiritual experience that puts you in touch with the last days of Christ," Tim said. "You don't want to miss it, so don't go anywhere on that day." I certainly didn't want to miss a miracle, and looked forward to it.

Good Friday was a beautiful day with a sun-drenched sky and red spots in all the fields: when spring descends on Rome bright red poppies appear everywhere: in fields, along freeways, even in garbage dumps. Nothing can stop them; they seem to bring an announcement of joy. "It doesn't seem like Good Friday," I remarked to Myles. We were on the upper terrace looking at a lily that had opened just that morning. "It should be dark and gloomy today to keep with the spirit of Good Friday." Myles agreed.

It was said that Brother Luigino would expire at about two p.m., three o'clock in Jerusalem. That morning at about 11:30

we were called up to Luigino's room. I wasn't sure what to expect as I walked up the stairs to the forbidden priestly floor. We lined up outside his door and when we were ushered in, we were permitted only to walk past his bed without pausing, to witness the experience for no more than thirty seconds. His room was small, with three windows on one side and a tiny closet. In the room were his personal doctor from the local village, a Franciscan priest who was said to be his spiritual director and another priest from the seminary. Brother Luigino, in his narrow bed against one wall, was wrapped in white: his sheets, his wrists, his bedclothes. His arms were rigid at his side and slightly raised, his eyes were closed, and he was moaning softly as if in pain.

I left the room thinking about the meaning of what I had just seen. A few doors down I passed the door of another priest from the community. I could hear that his television was on. I had just seen a mystical phenomenon and here was this priest, two doors down, watching a variety show. I wondered how he could be so disconnected from what was taking place. Didn't he believe in Luigino or care about spirituality? I didn't know him, but his indifference annoyed me.

After that visit to Luigino's room, we were free for the rest of the day. The Italian seminarians worried that when Brother Luigino expired, he might not come back to life. I didn't understand that fear, since this seemed to be an annual event. I stuck my head into the chapel; it was filled with the Italian seminarians praying for *Il Santo*. I went up to my room; glanced at my watch and noticed it was nearing two p.m., the moment of Brother Luigino's near-death experience.

I decided to go out on the roof terrace, a peaceful place for me, to enjoy the view. Stepping out, I saw that clouds had rolled in; in the distance the sky was blue. In fact, the sky was blue everywhere; only above San Vittorino and Tivoli was it dark and ominous. At two o'clock there was a thunderclap and torrents of rain began to fall; it seemed that the heavens were weeping only above the seminary. I sought refuge under the roofed walkway, asking myself if I could be witnessing a sign? After fifteen or twenty minutes the rain subsided and an hour later the sky was cloudless once more.

"That's the most impressive thing I've ever seen here," Myles said excitedly, stepping out onto the terrace. "A man can't control the weather!" News got around that Brother Luigino had expired and revived again. The seminary rejoiced. I felt happy: it was as if God had been made tangible through these events. I felt as if I was in the center of the world.

Easter had arrived and with it spring, a promise of new life. My distant patch of meadow was now vibrant green, spotted with red poppies that were everywhere, even around the seminary building. Excitement was in the air, and joy was flowing from three sources: Easter had come, the school year was nearing an end and plans were being made to return home for the summer.

The days grew longer and warmer, more pilgrims were coming to the seminary and we prepared for final exams and our departure. The exams didn't worry me as much as they had the first time, even though I still felt unsure of my level of expertise. But the anticipation of getting to return home to the U.S. was overwhelming and overshadowed everything.

Rome had retained its magic, but as spring wore on, I found myself daydreaming of the giant redwoods, of Yosemite National Park, of the beaches, the river running through my hometown of Modesto. "It's significant," said Father Tim, a newly ordained American priest I was saying my confession to one evening, "that what you miss most is the land, not particular faces."

His words hurt. Was something wrong with me? Was I missing the wrong thing? Perhaps I missed the environment more than the people because after my mother's death I felt close to no one. My family seemed like strangers; my interests were not theirs, they knew nothing of my life here, and they didn't seem interested. Family ties are simply a biological accident, I told myself. Yes, I did miss California, especially the redwoods. I would go see the redwoods when I got home.

Several weeks after Easter there was a knocking at the door of my cubicle and Brother Luigino's short Italian assistant stuck his head into my room: "*Marco, Fratel Luigino e' libero; vieni*"—"Mark, Brother Luigino will see you now; come." Quickly I gathered my list of things to talk about and headed downstairs.

A new building had been completed for Brother Luigino to receive visitors. I was led upstairs into a medium-sized room divided by a large grill as before. The assistant left us. This was the second time I had seen *Il Santo* in private; this time I came prepared with a list of topics. I wanted to speak with him about my family situation, my mother's death and my fears for the future.

He again invited me to sit with him on the same side of the grill and he listened as I went down my list. The advice he gave me was simple: my mother was looking down, watching over me; I should pray at home and soon I would be back in Italy at the end of the summer. I should continue on this road; it was the right one for me.

After this talk, he embraced me. I rejoiced at being embraced by a saint. "*Mi vuoi bene?*—Do you love me?" he asked.

"*Molto*—a lot," I said. I began to feel aroused by the embrace: no one had ever embraced me like that before. I fought the arousal, hoping that he wouldn't notice it. As I had the first time, I ascribed it to my own lack of progress in the spiritual life, because the embrace of the saint was as far from sexuality as the moon from the sun. I felt ashamed of my reaction, but glad the encounter had taken place. Now I could return to America with renewed hope and strength.

It is easier than one might think not to love oneself. When someone showed me love and affection, I was elated because it was a sign that I was lovable, something that was not clear to me in those years. The void I felt was temporarily filled; it was as if I could value myself again because Luigino had held me. Since he had such spiritual gifts that he could see deeply into others, I must be lovable. But why does such love shown by others never last? Why do those positive feelings evaporate? I had not yet experienced a healthy relationship in which one learns to love oneself through the eyes of another. I found myself stuck at the sign just like those pilgrims who came to catch a glimpse of *Il Santo*.

Over the next few weeks, our excitement increased as we made final preparations to return home. Four of us planned to take the train to London to catch stand-by flights to our various cities from there. Marcus joined our group. He had brought many books to Rome the previous fall, few of which he had opened. When I came to Italy I had packed fairly lightly, but still my suitcases had proven to be too heavy, so I resolved to bring only a few things back. I hoped Marcus would do the same.

Final exams at the Angelicum went uneventfully. I couldn't get over my dissatisfaction that I had learned so little even though I had passed the courses. Was it the fault of the European teaching method, in which 200 or so students hear lectures together all term and are expected to demonstrate what they have learned in a ten-minute oral exam? Was it the fault of the seminary schedule that left little time to study? Or was it my fault for not doing enough outside research? I resolved to work through Coplestone's *History of Philosophy* on my return. Goal-setting always gave me a sense of peace; I could look forward to solving the problem instead of feeling like a victim.

The day before we left, I was so looking forward to going home that I could hardly sleep that night. As I stood at the window looking at the stars, I felt that the same stars in California would somehow connect me to this place.

"Where's Marcus?" I asked Dave as we raced towards our train at the station.

"He's lugging his suitcases about a block down there," Dave said, irritated. When I asked whether we should we go back to help him, Dave said, "Hey, you pack 'em, you carry 'em."

Marcus caught up with us, dragging two suitcases. He said they were filled with books that he might need over the summer. I tried to lift one of his suitcases; it must have weighed about ninety pounds. "Okay," I said, "I'll save you a place on the train." I could feel his anger, but I decided to ignore it.

When we landed in New York, I left a message on my father's answering machine that I was arriving in San Francisco at five p.m., and asked him to pick me up at the baggage claim for TWA flight 447. Just several more hours and I would be home

"*M'hijo!*" screamed Marcus's mother as we left the plane in San Francisco. Marcus's father was always very quiet but his eyes were full of tears. They hugged him and his mother said, "I've made all of your favorite foods for dinner, and your cousins want to see you, but I told them to wait until tomorrow." She asked me whether I needed a ride home. And, "Where are your parents?"

Where were my parents? "No, they're coming," I told her. "They're always late. I'll wait in the baggage claim."

It was about a hundred miles from my home to the airport. I waited in the baggage claim for an hour, an hour and a half. Finally I picked up the phone and called home. Dad answered. "Hello, Mark. We didn't come because the flight number you gave us was from London to New York."

"Why didn't you call the airlines to find out what the connecting flight number was? I told you it arrives at five o'clock. on TWA; that's all you needed," I said.

"We didn't want to go all the way to San Francisco and not know where you were. So we decided to wait until you called. We'll leave and pick you up at the baggage claim there. Don't go anywhere."

Another hour passed, two hours, three hours; I was furious. It had been a year since I'd seen them. I was fuming when, after four hours, I heard my father: "Mark, there you are!" He shook my hand. "You must be tired," my stepmother commented as I got into the car.

"Exhausted," I replied, with my head down. I felt displaced, undervalued, unwelcome.

"How was your trip?" came the obligatory inquiry.

"Tiring. I'll tell you about it."

They didn't say anything more. I wondered why they didn't ask me about my year, what I did, what I saw, what I experienced. In fact, they *never* asked me about my time in the seminary. Did my faith make them feel uncomfortable? If so, I thought, it was their loss. By the time we arrived home, it was late.

"Mark, if you're hungry, I can get dinner ready in a while here. I haven't had time all day," my stepmother said.

"Sure. I'm not real hungry."

I lugged my suitcases back to my old room and opened the door. It was no longer a bedroom at all but seemed to be a storage room; there were clothes and papers all over the bed and the floor.

"I've put you in your brother's old room," she called from the kitchen. I went to my brother's room, and put my suitcases in the closet. My father, sitting down in the living room to relax before dinner, called to me too: "Mark, am I going to get any work out of you while you're home?"

I leaned my head against the wall. Why, oh why, had I come? I hadn't been in the house for fifteen minutes and already I regretted having returned. Nothing had changed.

Over the next few days, as I shopped, spoke with acquaintances, watched television, I felt like an alien. The society in which I had lived had changed; it seemed pathetic, ridiculous and superficial, dominated by stupid computer games and TV shows. I felt a stranger not only in my home but also in my country. I yearned for a sense of belonging, but it was clear that I wouldn't find it here.

Marcus phoned to tell me, "My mom doesn't want me to work this summer so I can spend more time with my family. They're going to cover my plane fare." I, on the other hand, had no choice; I needed to earn my plane fare and was soon commuting to the pear-packing plant. If the season lasted, I could make just enough for my round-trip fare.

As the days went by in those first weeks, I found myself longing to be back in Italy. But while I was there, I had longed to be back here. I was confused. Where did I belong? After work I would drive to the river to be alone and stare at the drifting water; it seemed to be the only place where I could find peace. By mid-July the fruit-packing season had dried up, but I had made 600 dollars—enough to go to Europe and back again if I flew standby. I decided to return early so I could do some traveling before reporting to the seminary on September first. I could make my own adventure.

———

"I don't know if I feel comfortable leaving you at the airport all night when you're not sure you'll get on a flight," my father remarked, as we drove to the airport in San Francisco.

I wondered if he was sincere. He seemed to be playing the role of a concerned parent, but at that point it didn't matter to me. My plan was to fly standby to London, sightsee for a few days, then make my way to Rome and explore the city for a little while. After that I planned to spend the rest of the time before September first in Florence. I had 200 dollars in my pocket and no credit card.

"I'll be fine, Dad, I've done this before."

At the airport the ticket agent assured me that I would get on since the plane was fairly empty. My father again shook hands with me before dashing back to his life, while I looked forward to mine.

To Marcus it was incomprehensible that I would return to Europe early. His parents could not get enough of him. I hadn't known such affection since my mother's death. I had learned to live for other things and thought Marcus's attachment to his family to be limiting; he was unwilling to explore the world or to take any risks. I thought he was childish and spoiled. I was leaving my old life; the world was waiting for me.

I didn't know much about European history and culture, so when I arrived in London I wasn't sure where to go or what to see. I rented a room the size of a closet and wandered around the city, stopping at Westminster Abbey, Westminster Cathedral and enjoying the street musicians who were everywhere that summer. I took a train to Oxford to visit the university and discovered a wonderful bookstore where I purchased a Greek lexicon. My money was going fast, the city was expensive, and it was time I left.

I had a feeling of coming home as I boarded the train to Rome. I had done this before, I knew how to do it and I was excited to be on my own. I hadn't spoken to anyone in days, but I didn't mind. As I watched the countryside whirl by, I was absorbed in my thoughts. I didn't feel lonely. I didn't expect more human closeness than I had experienced in my life thus far. Here on the road, I found myself absorbed, silent for days, sometimes excited, but not lonely.

The main train station in Rome was always a bustle of confusion. It was full of people but there was no one there one could trust. I kept one hand on my wallet, and walked out into the hot sun to the grand plaza. I could finally explore the city without a schedule or someone telling me what to do; I was on an adventure.

Near the Stazione Termini there were many places to stay for no more than ten dollars a night: cheap *pensioni* and dreary hotels. I followed the directions in my budget guide through some residential streets and rang the bell of the first place listed on that page. It was in a large palazzo with about six floors, the private home of a family of six, two daughters and two dogs. I was given the keys to the front door. The family seemed strangely trusting. In my room were six beds; the bathroom was down the hall. Several backpacks lay on some of the beds. I chose a bed, hoping that my belongings would be safe. The place was not ideal, but I was happy: I was not accountable to anyone. I was free to explore the "Forbidden City."

I headed off in the direction of the Coliseum, stepped into the Roman Forum, and walked up the Palatine to the remains of the emperor's palace, impressive even in their ruined state. At the Coliseum, I felt myself to be one of the Roman spectators watching the games below amid the roar of the crowd. I spent the rest of that day sitting in the Coliseum, thinking, imagining, listening to the ancient world.

The next morning I visited the Vatican museum. I found it especially confusing as I wandered through a large corridor filled with marble animals of every type and time period, jumbled together without explanations. But when I walked into the hall of paintings, I was enraptured by Spanish Baroque art. There was one piece that made me stop and linger: a painting of priests and nuns being martyred for their faith. The scene was calm but dramatic, sad and beautiful. I was enjoying myself here. Even in my ignorance, the art and culture of this place flooded my emotions. I began to feel that Rome was "my" city; I felt a familiarity growing that would eventually become my life.

The train from Rome to Florence took no time at all and I quickly found budget lodging near the station. When I arrived it was nearly evening. I took a relaxed stroll around the city as the sun was setting. The panorama took on an orange hue; the bridges were reflected in the golden Arno, the rooftops, the cathedral dome and the sky reflected yellow and crimson like a Sicilian blood orange. I stopped in the street to breathe it in. It was so beautiful. For the first time I longed to share this with someone. But Marcus was happy in Modesto with his loving mother and I had no other real friends. There was no one to share it with.

After I had dined at a sidewalk café on delicious green lasagna, I wandered for hours in the Florentine night; the city was filled with tourists and I was sometimes embarrassed by loud Americans in flashy clothing. I arrived at the cathedral to see the gates of paradise and spent a long time looking at each scene. Though I knew little of Florentine history its beauty was enough.

Returning to my *pensione*, as I passed two young women strolling by, an Italian man in front of me stopped and openly ogled them. I had seen this before, in Rome. Italian men always stopped to gawk at women's behinds. Men didn't act like that in America, at least respectable men didn't. Italians, I thought, have no respect for women; everything is reduced to lust. Later I would view this differently, to see it as the Italian appreciation of beauty. It is this that draws them to take long walks to enjoy the nice weather, to spend an entire evening in a restaurant for a meal, or to save money to buy one good piece of clothing instead of five or six cheaper ones.

It was hot and stuffy when I toured the main art museum, the Uffizi, the next day. I had never seen so many paintings in one place. I was surprised that there was no climate control; the windows were open; the sun shining through the windows made it difficult sometimes to see the paintings. I went from room to room, enjoying myself, until after two hours I ran out of energy and wanted only to go to bed.

But I thought this might be the last time I could come here, so I forced myself to go to every single room. The experience became painful. I felt no hunger, just fatigue. Hours later, when I had seen the last room, I crawled out of the museum towards my pensione, forced myself to eat a sandwich and fell into bed until evening. I was exhausted but happy. I was on a great journey.

Wandering around the next day, I was surprised at how

small Florence was; it seemed a village compared with Rome. Art was everywhere: as I took my long walks I could not find any place, any section, any street, that was ugly. Florence was as beautiful as it appeared in the dreamy soft backgrounds of many Renaissance paintings. I spent only three days there, but I was bewitched until the day I had to leave.

YEAR 2

Signs Along the Path

———

As THE BUS SPED TOWARD San Vittorino from the train station, I gazed out the window at the beautiful countryside and at the litter along the road. Italy, the land of contrasts. There was a prostitute about 100 yards away who lifted up her dress; the driver stopped the bus to try to coax her to do it again. They flirted for a good five minutes while the passengers waited. She refused to give him another peek so he drove off. Rome seemed to be that one place in which sensuality and faith not only coexist but even intertwine. For an American like myself this seemed bizarre; to me piety meant giving up pleasure, especially sensual pleasure.

The longer I stayed in Italy the more I wondered if perhaps humanity and divinity, the "flesh" and the "spirit," could be intertwined and flourish together. Perhaps human weakness was not an obstacle to God's presence. In fact, perhaps these weaknesses were doors through which He enters into life, into real life. Could it be that God's love does not depend on being good, but just on being oneself? Bemused, I was jolted back into reality when the bus driver announced, "San Vittorino!"

I walked through the village and up the path towards the shrine. It was 1979 and I was now in my second year in Rome. As I rounded the bend, I spotted a group of seminarians. There were fresh faces: fifteen or so Americans, a sprinkling of Canadians and twice as many Italians as the year before.

Each summer Brother Luigino invited some Italians to spend a few weeks with him in the countryside near his hometown in Tuscany. He used this opportunity to steer them towards the seminary. Virtually all the Italian seminarians had been recruited in this way.

The new Italians formed a varied group: two brothers, Antonio and Mario, who had been among the top wrestlers in Italy; Sergio, a simple uneducated man from Brother Luigino's town; Mario from Naples, a smelly man with a big stomach and a bigger heart, and others as varied as Italy itself. A few came from very religious backgrounds, but most did not. For them, Brother Luigino represented the discovery of faith.

The new Americans at the seminary were simply very pious young men. I spent the afternoon chatting and trying to get to know a few of them. They loved to talk about religion, but seemed to have no other interests. "What about these guys?" I asked Chris from Michigan, who was in my class. "They're so pious that you can't have any other conversation with them except about the lives of the saints. I find them boring." Chris just laughed.

"How was your summer, Larry?" I asked, somewhat regretting the way I had treated Killjoy the previous year.

"Good," he answered with his broad smile.

"What did you do?"

"Oh, helped my mom, went to church, things like that."

What kind of life does this guy have, I asked myself. Doesn't he do anything interesting at all? What about his friends?

"What about you?" he asked.

"Worked, spent time with friends; then I went to London and Florence," I said proudly. I resolved to try to get along better with Larry this year.

Steve arrived from Los Angeles a few days later. He was tall, tanned and balding; a very intelligent but undisciplined man who was searching for some structure in his life after being kicked out of college. He had been in my class the year before. We were not especially close, but we had some friends in common in California.

After the meal we went outside for our usual walk; it was hot, so most of us immediately sought shade. When he saw Steve, Brother Luigino called him over. We all sat underneath a tall umbrella-shaped pine tree. "I received a telephone call about you," Luigino said to Steve, who laughed nervously. "A telephone call saying you were in trouble, asking me to pray."

When he said "*telefonata*" he motioned upward as if saying it was some divine communication. "I was asked to pray for you and so I did, that you might be delivered."

Steve didn't say much; he was usually very talkative but now he seemed embarrassed. My curiosity increased when I noticed that Luigino kept nodding and smiling at Steve for the rest of the day. At the first opportunity. I asked Steve what that was all about.

"Let's go take a walk, Mark, and I'll explain it all to you . . . I got back to Rome a week before I showed up at San Vittorino, and one night I went to a seedy part of town where there are lots of prostitutes. Well, there was one who was not very pretty but she asked me for twenty bucks for sex, so I went for it. She led me to a dirty little room; we walked by a man who I think was her pimp. We get to the room and I'm getting ready to have sex and she goes in the bathroom to get ready. So here I am on the bed, undressed, and she comes out. Well, *she* turned out to be a *he*.

"He still wanted to have sex but I said, 'No, no no.' So he says he's still going to keep my money and leaves the room. I get dressed and still have my shoes in my hand when I go downstairs and see him standing on the street talking with the pimp, holding my twenty bucks. So I grab the money out of his hand and run all the way down the street, barefoot, while they're cursing and chasing me. I outran them. So, in the end, it was like God was playing a joke on me. Now how Brother Luigino knew about that, I don't know."

The story seemed like a confirmation of the other things I had heard about Luigino. God seemed to work through him.

——

October 15th marked the beginning of the new term and I was more confident because I could actually understand the Italian lectures. I developed a note-taking shorthand, partly in English and partly in Italian. Some courses were interesting but most of them bored me. The professors at the Angelicum were the top scholars in their fields but most had no pedagogical skills at all. They seemed disconnected, unaware of the students in front of them, who were seminarians from various religious groups and orders from many nations.

The wildest group were the Syrians, who were always energetic and full of fun. They could often be seen laughing and joking in the corridors and playing table tennis in the basement. The most rigid were a group called the Legionnaires of Christ, a Spanish order with mostly Spanish and American seminarians. They always stood until the professor entered the room, never engaged in conversation with anyone who was not a Legionnaire and, when class ended, filed to their waiting bus where they sat in silence.

We seminarians from San Vittorino were called the Oblates because the seminary belonged to the Oblates of the Virgin Mary. We lived in a strict seminary environment, but our attitudes were rather relaxed. Members of our group might be found praying in the chapel, studying in the library or cutting class to see the city. As the weeks passed we settled into the school routine, taking notes, going over the material at home, doing some outside readings on the history of philosophy, beginning research papers, as well as adhering to the seminary schedule.

A conflict broke out between two groups in the seminary over prayer. It was the custom that the rosary be recited in the vans to and from school. Some Americans objected to this, saying they needed the commuting time to study. The rosary supporters called the others "atheists"; it grew into a conflict between the "atheists" and the "believers." Personally, I didn't care either way. Usually on the way home from school in the van, I dozed off and on the way to school sometimes I joined in the prayers and sometimes I didn't. There was also the practice of adding on prayers at the end of the rosary. Bill from Oakland, a short man with a limp, was in the seminary chapel every day doing the Stations of the Cross. He seemed to fill his life with dozens of devotions and pious practices.

At the conclusion of each rosary, he would raise his voice and say, "Let us offer one Our Father, Hail Mary, and Glory Be for the Holy Father," followed by, "Let us offer one Hail Mary for vocations," then, "Let us offer one Hail Mary for the souls in purgatory." It seemed the prayers were getting longer and longer with these additions. After a tiring school day, everyone wanted some quiet before arriving home. One day in the van, at the conclusion of the rosary, Armando, an Italian seminarian from Rome, added: "Let's say one Hail Mary so no one will add any more Hail Marys." Everyone laughed except Bill.

"From now on," Fr. Malacelli said at a conference, "there will be one van that travels in silence, so that those who want to study on the way to school can do so. And there will be no more calling atheists those who ride in that van."

Malacelli was a practical man with short, graying hair and a red face. He was highstrung, often screaming with rage and minutes later bursting into laughter. He created a tense atmosphere; no one dared to cross him or break his rules. He relied more on commonsense than on intellectual ability to guide himself and the seminary. I feared, respected and disliked him.

The shrine continued to draw busloads of pilgrims, who would have Mass in the washing-machine-turbine church. I found the interior ugly. Black marble everywhere created a dark atmosphere, there was an enormous starburst tabernacle in the middle, a huge statue of Our Lady of Fatima on one side and a larger-than-life crucifix on the other. Religious and contemporary art was jumbled together. The altar was in the center with seating all around it so that if one looked up during a service, people on the other side would be staring directly back.

The Italian visitors, fascinated by the seminarians, gaped at us from across the church. Italians tended to stare in a way that Americans hesitate to do. They seemed to see us seminarians as the inside group around *Il Santo*, the ones who knew all the secrets and saw all the miracles. But not every pilgrim was pious. One night, as a seminarian from Michigan was leaving the church service, an Italian woman grabbed his crotch. "When she grabbed me I was shocked, but I thought about it later and figured that she wanted to see if it was still there," he said, with a wink.

Once a month there was a religious procession: hundreds of people would descend on San Vittorino and Brother Luigino would lead the group around the grounds, through the village and back again to the church, reciting the rosary and singing hymns. So much attention was on Luigino that I wondered if the pilgrims came to pray to God or just to see him. They knelt on the ground when they recited the "Glory be to the Father." Malacelli had forbidden the seminarians to do that; he wanted to avoid any appearance of fanaticism. I was just glad not to get my pants dirty.

In this religious procession, Luigino moved forward surrounded by the seminarians who acted as his bodyguards. When visitors tried to approach, Maurizio chased them away. But this day no one was invading his space; everyone was reciting the prayers blasting from the loudspeaker on top of the turbine church. As we rounded a turn I noticed someone peering through the bushes to get a glimpse of *Il Santo*. I wondered who that fanatic was, and what he expected to see? As we drew nearer, I saw that it was that same Franciscan priest whom I had seen last Good Friday in Luigino's room, the priest said to be Luigino's confessor. How odd, I thought, he seems to be more fixated than the rest, glaring out between the branches of a shrub. If he really was Luigino's confessor, why was he was acting so fanatical?

Later that night, after our dinner of soup, fried eggs and bread, I went outside with the others and my stomach started to ache as it did fairly often. This time the pain was unbearable so I left the others on the terrace and went inside. We were not allowed to go up to our rooms until 9:30 p.m. and it was only 8:45. I didn't know what to do. I waited by the stairs, clutching my stomach. What could be wrong with me? Finally I decided that enough was enough and went up to my room to lie down. That seemed to help. After ten o'clock I heard the others coming up to their rooms. As the hours passed the pain subsided and, as had happened before, when I woke up, the ache was gone.

———

The leaves had given way to brittle branches and the air grew cold as the seminary routine engulfed us. There were not enough hours in the day, every free moment had to be filled with study, and still we were always behind. The Americans took their schoolwork more seriously than the Italians did. At the Angelicum we studied the work of Thomas Aquinas in most of our classes. Aquinas's system of philosophy and theology was based on Aristotelian thought. He saw no contradiction between faith and reason and used the one to explore the other. When Aquinas had almost completed his masterpiece, the *Summa Theologica*, he had a vision in which he comprehended something about God, something so much greater than reason, so much beyond the human intellect, that he stopped writing, saying, "Compared with what I experienced, what I have written is all straw."

The Italian seminarians seized on this as a justification for not studying. There was one resident, in fact, named Sergio,

who was almost illiterate. The afternoons were to be devoted
to schoolwork, but I noticed that not only did he never study,
he never stayed in his room. If I went downstairs, there he was;
when I went on the terrace, there he was. He was everywhere
trying to kill time, trying to avoid hitting the books. This attitude of the Italians bothered me and explained why there are
some incredibly incompetent professionals in Italian institutions. Most of the Americans understood that learning, not only
spirituality, is valuable, so we dedicated ourselves to both.

The schedule was broken one day by an announcement
from Jeff, a seminarian from Michigan: "On the feast of the
Immaculate Conception the Madonna appears to Brother
Luigino every year and blesses the objects in his room. So if
you have anything for her to bless, give them to me and I'll
make sure they're put in his room." Jeff had huge hands, the
thickest glasses I've ever seen and was always making rosaries.
I put a stack of holy cards and my rosary into a bag and gave
it to Jeff.

I smelled something new when I came down the stairwell
the next morning, December eighth, the Immaculate Conception. A flower scent always came from Brother Luigino, but
this was not a perfume smell, it seemed fuller: the fragrance
itself and its intensity had changed. People called it the "odor
of sanctity." It seemed stronger on one side of the stairwell; it
seemed to be streaming down to the foot of the stairs.

We had to go to school that day, but we came back to the
seminary, eager to hear about Luigino's experiences, to get a
report of his "vision" the night before. After lunch I joined a
group huddled around *Il Santo*. An extremely strong scent of
roses was coming from him. "What did the Madonna say?"
Maurizio asked him.

Brother Luigino smiled; he seemed reluctant to tell. But he
did say that he saw a woman made of rays of light, rays that
fell on the objects the seminarians had sent to his room. It was
extraordinary to think that the seminary had had such a visitor

that night while we slept. When I received my rosary and holy cards back a few days later, they emitted that same scent, which lasted for several weeks. Excited, I felt I was at the center of the most special place on earth, where God touched humans.

Over the following weeks, groups continued to arrive at San Vittorino to pray and see *Il Santo*. One day an old woman approached, dressed all in black like most elderly Italian widows. (It seemed strange to me that one would wear black for one's whole life after one had lost one's husband.) She was stooped over, wrinkled, skeletal. When she was about ten feet away, she suddenly broke into a song to the Virgin Mary. I wanted to laugh because she was off-key and the situation struck me as funny. I looked at Luigino; he was smiling too, but then we all realized that she was serious, that this was an act expressing her faith, so we listened seriously.

When she finished singing, Brother Luigino thanked her and we all walked off. Then he turned to us and said, "If you get married, that is what your wife will look like some day. Beauty fades. It is better to not marry; it is better to be celibate like us. Could you imagine waking up to that every day?" He motioned at her.

Marcus and I drifted away from Brother Luigino's group and walked towards the seminary. Marcus was outraged: "That's somebody's grandmother! That could be my grandmother! How could he say such a thing? For all the reasons to be celibate that's the worst I've ever heard!"

I had to agree. On more than one occasion, in fact, Brother Luigino would repeat his opinion of marriage as something tainted and dirty. He couched sexuality in distasteful terms, as something sordid and evil. This struck me one day as Maurizio told us a story about Brother Luigino's encounter with a terrible creature one night in downtown Rome. This was a monster, a sort of huge clamshell with legs, trying to capture him. Once in its grip, his life would be ended. The horrible creature pursued him through dark Roman alleys and streets. Panic-stricken, he knocked on doors for help, but no one responded.

Describing the creature to me, Maurizio used some Italian words I was not familiar with; I asked him to explain in simpler Italian. "The creature," he said, "was about ten feet tall and had the form of the female sexual organ." When he told me this, I didn't know whether to be shocked or to laugh, so I tried to do neither. A giant vagina was chasing *Il Santo* through the streets of Rome! When I got back to my room I had to laugh out loud at the scene this called up. But later I began to wonder how one could be so in touch with the divine and still have ideas like that.

On another evening, Brother Luigino, talking about his youth and his time in the seminary, told us, "There was a German fellow in the seminary. One evening I walked into the common bathroom and there he was, completely naked! That was not right and it disturbed me very much. In fact, I was so disturbed I had to go outside and walk and walk for hours before I was able to get to sleep."

As I heard him describe this, I wondered if I had misunderstood. Was he saying that he had a sexual attraction to this German that he struggled with before going to bed? If he was indeed saying he was homosexual, why didn't the Italians react? I was perplexed. I too had struggled with these tendencies but had buried them deep beneath my emotional life so that I did not have to consider them. What was Brother Luigino saying here? Perhaps it was the language barrier that prevented me from understanding him. I didn't dare ask anyone about it.

One cold February day an announcement came: "Brother Luigino, telephone!" This was significant, since he never received telephone calls. What could this be? After a few minutes he returned and told us, "That was Mother Theresa. She will come here to visit tomorrow morning."

"But how did you understand her since you don't speak English and she doesn't speak Italian?" Maurizio asked.

"When we spoke we both understood each other," Luigino said. "When all was said that needed to be said we stopped understanding each other."

I had heard of Mother Theresa when I was in high school; her work with the poor in India had made headlines and yet she remained a simple, humble woman. I had seen her nuns in Rome on various occasions and always felt inspired by their dedication and faith. And now Mother Theresa herself was coming to my seminary on her own initiative! But why? I couldn't wait to find out. Fr. Malacelli refused to let us miss school the next day to see her, so by the time we returned to the seminary, Mother Theresa and her sisters had already come and gone. We had to wait to hear about it from the only ones who had been there: Brother Luigino and Maurizio. "Maurizio, you tell them what you saw and heard," Luigino encouraged him.

"She came to visit with you—Brother Luigino—to ask for prayers for her mission. She said that God desires a spiritual union between her religious order and ours. She asked us to send priests to India to work with her nuns."

One of the Americans asked, "And what did you say to that?"

Brother Luigino replied: "I told her we will go with Gary." Gary was an American doctor and seminarian studying theology in Rome, who had worked with Mother Theresa's nuns in India.

"Wow!" I said to myself, back in my room. "A spiritual union!"

I was excited to see it confirmed once more that I was in the middle of exciting events, powerful enough to influence history. I had wanted my life to become something great and I was in the ideal place for this to happen. Again, I felt grateful to be here. Notwithstanding some of my difficulties—stomach pains, occasional depression, longing to be far away—I never found myself doubting that this was the right path. I was certain that I was exactly where I was supposed to be. My life could become something great if I lived for something great, like Mother Theresa, like Brother Luigino and many before them. That afternoon I felt happy, privileged, and excited.

Months went by and my Italian improved considerably so that I could follow the philosophy lectures without difficulty. At the seminary my friendship deepened with Amadeo, the shrill-voiced Italian from Belluno, and with Livinus and Jude, from Nigeria. It seemed that this year would end like the year before: growing excitement, Easter, final exams, and departure for home. However, at the beginning of May something happened that shook all of us up completely. Summer vacation was approaching, we were making travel plans and putting outlines together for the final exams, when Marcus received a phone call from Modesto during lunch. He didn't return to the table or go outside afterward. I went to look for him and found him in his room, packing a suitcase. He was distraught.

"My brother's dead," he said. "I have to go."

Though Marcus and I had drifted apart, I knew him better than anyone else. I knew his family and I had met his brother.

"What are you going to do?" I asked.

"What am I supposed to do? I'm going home. I'll come back and take the exams."

The next forty-eight hours were like a whirlwind. Marcus told his professors, the rector of the seminary and everyone else involved in his life in Rome, that he needed to go home immediately and everyone, including the airline, was willing to help. Two days later he was on a plane. I was stunned and felt very bad, especially for his mother.

Others in the seminary asked me about it. "What did his brother die from?"

"Marcus said he was killed."

"Murdered?"

"Before he left he told me that his brother had been poisoned. I don't know any other details."

Marcus never did talk about it, but several years later I learned that his brother had died of a drug overdose.

I wondered whether Marcus would return. He was so attached to his family and had always been less caught up than I by the magic of Rome. But he did believe that it was God's will that he be there and to him God's will was something external and static, detached from any human emotion. Marcus would not go against what he perceived as God's will even if it made him miserable. So chances are, I thought, he'll be back. I would find out when I got home in about four weeks. In the meantime I needed to focus on my final exams and on how I was going to get back to California. Dave was able to find some cheap flights from Rome to California through a contact he made in the Pan Am office, so we didn't have to make the trek to London. I planned to leave right after my exams and to come back early to travel on my own.

Again, as the time to leave approached, I was eager to be returning to California, but my excitement was tempered by the death of Marcus's brother and by my family situation. I couldn't wait to get back to my own country and culture but to be back in my parents' house was less appealing. I had no other place to go.

One day, Steve from Los Angeles said, "Mark, why don't you come down to L.A. with me for a few days and I'll drive you up to Modesto? You can stay at my parents' house." After a year I still didn't know Steve well, but some things were obvious: he was outspoken, opinionated, brilliant, undisciplined, insensitive and interesting. I accepted.

Final exams passed without a problem this time. I was less nervous since I knew I was prepared. On the heels of the finals came the day of departure; I was excited as we boarded the public transportation to the airport and arrived in Los Angeles without any trains or London detours. By the time we arrived at Steve's house from the airport, I couldn't see straight. I could never sleep on flights, and I felt all the stress of the previous month. I was exhausted, but it was good to be back in California: the sky seemed bigger, the cities brighter, the colors of nature more vibrant.

Steve's family lived in a suburban house with a front lawn and a swimming pool. After being in Italy I really liked this place. The plan was for me to spend a few days here, after which Steve would drive me up to Modesto. But I didn't feel comfortable. I didn't really know these people and the bond between Steve and me was based only on the fact that we were both from California. I awoke the next morning to a noisy and animated conversation in the dining room. They were all loud and outspoken, as was Steve; everyone was talking at the same time and nobody was listening. They were passionate about politics and were discussing the candidates in an upcoming election. I didn't hear Steve's voice, and I felt awkward leaving my room, so after I got up I stayed there and read.

By late morning I was regretting having come there. "Where's Mark?" I heard a female voice inquire. A few minutes later his sister knocked at my door. "Mark," she said, "Steve's not here, but come on out. He went out with some friends. I think he'll be back soon." I ate some breakfast and sat with these strangers, until a few hours later a car drove up. Steve hurried past me into his room, threw some of his clothes into a bag, went into the kitchen and picked up some food, then rushed past me. "Sorry," he said, "I can't take you up to Modesto." He went out the front door to join his buddies who were waiting for him.

I flew to Modesto; my father met me at the local airport and gave me my annual handshake. I found the situation at home much the same as the year before, as I had expected. The river and the wooded areas near my parents' house became my refuge, the only place I felt happy. Whenever I could, I slipped out alone and watched the birds and the water.

I had left several messages for Marcus, but he hadn't responded. I needed money to fly back to Italy, so I went to work at the orchard every day, packing pears, dreaming of Rome, wanting more out of life than I could find here.

"Dad, do you have any stamps?" I called from my bedroom one evening.

"Check the study," was the answer.

The study had been my bedroom; the bed was now covered with papers; odds and ends were all over the floor, there were several file cabinets, and a closet overflowing with my stepmother's clothes. On a desk, under a mountain of folders, books, and envelopes, I spied the stamp container—but alas, no stamps. I was scrounging in a drawer when something blue caught my eye; the color of the aerogrammes that I had sent home. I found a stack of them; two or three were opened, but the rest of those that I had written to my parents that year had not even been opened. I resolved never to write to them again. I wondered why I always looked forward to returning home when I was never happy there.

While I was working at the orchard, I had time to think about the past year and about my present situation. I found my hometown suffocating; its horizons were too narrow. "Once a cow town, always a cow town," people would say. Yet in Rome I longed for California. I had only two options: Modesto or Rome. The choice was simple.

Weeks later Marcus returned my phone call. He didn't volunteer any information about his brother's death and I didn't think it was right to ask. Marcus's main concern seemed to be for his mother, who kept repeating that she wanted to die. I asked how his father was doing.

"I don't know, he doesn't say anything, he's just quiet."

"How are you?"

"I just feel numb, I don't feel anything."

I offered any moral support I could give, knowing that my words rang hollow. His family had been struck with a tragedy. His mother said that she would never be happy again; her life would never be the same. The lives of Marcus and his family had been devastated. I wondered, "If I died tomorrow, would anyone's life be affected or changed?" The answer was obvious. Even though I knew I was on the right road, I was not loved. My life didn't really matter to anyone. At 21 years old I felt alone in the world: there was no one there for me. But I didn't allow these feelings to overwhelm me. They were simply my reality. I packed these thoughts and emotions away and put them in a corner of my life, hoping that they would leave me undisturbed.

That summer I didn't see much of Marcus but he reassured me that he would return to Rome, although later than I would, and that he would fill me in there on what was happening at home. I offered him my support again; I didn't know what else to do.

Soon I had earned the necessary $600 for my airfare and I prepared for my return.

Pandora's Box

———·

I HAD NEVER REALLY THOUGHT ABOUT entering a religious order. I had chosen to go to San Vittorino because it was reputed to be a solid seminary, the classes were held at a pontifical university in Rome and there was a saint in residence. I was turned off by what I had heard about American seminaries. For decades they had been run like monasteries, with the students completely separated from the world, and theology was a static discipline. Change was necessary: students needed experience working directly with people and theology needed to grow and adapt. So this was a divisive time. Progressive elements who accused Church leaders and seminaries of being too "pre-Vatican II" were considered by conservatives to be traitors to Catholicism.

This political infighting went on within the Catholic Church, especially in the United States. At the time I reached the age to enter the seminary, these institutions were reacting to everything that had gone before, especially in the field of theology. If I followed a path to the priesthood I did not want to be in the middle of an ideological battlefield. I had decided years before that if I wasn't able to get to Rome, I wouldn't follow the road to the priesthood. So here I was, in a seminary run by the Oblates of the Virgin Mary and about to begin my third year, called the Novitiate, a full year dedicated to studying the spirituality of one's religious order, working on his prayer life, and preparing to take the three vows of chastity, poverty and obedience.

The Oblates had just purchased a new Novitiate house on the Janiculum Hill in Rome. It was a beautiful place, built as a convent, with thirty individual rooms, a good-sized garden, a kitchen as big as a thimble and a small chapel that could not hold all of us. This was a turning point and a new beginning on my road. Our Novitiate group would become more closely knit that year. I knew that 1980 would be one of my most important years as I prepared formally to dedicate my life to God.

After the first week a routine was set. A typical day consisted of Mass in the morning followed by breakfast, then a conference given by Father Boroni who was the Novice Master. Then an afternoon conference was followed by a holy hour (prayers and meditation) and dinner. Unlike the seminary in San Vittorino, in the Novitiate house we had no nuns preparing our meals or doing our laundry, so I volunteered to work in the kitchen. I found I had a largely undiscovered talent for cooking, and friendships sprang up in the kitchen. But even though I enjoyed the externals of the community, I was becoming aware of a suffering deep within me. I continued to feel that my life, my very existence, didn't really matter much to anyone. I felt alone.

After some weeks in the Novitiate it became clear that Father Boroni's conferences were less than enthralling. We studied the documents of Vatican II on the religious life as well as the writings of the founder of the Oblates, Father Lanteri. I found some of the documents interesting, but Boroni used repetition to get his points across and gave few real examples. I started to suspect that our Novice Master had a limited experience of life. I noticed this particularly one evening when he came back from hearing the confessions of a convent of nuns in Rome, something he did for them twice monthly.

"Did you hear what Father Boroni said when he got back?" I asked Amadeo. "He said that it was fun for him, that it is what he enjoys the most. In other words, for him, fun is going to a convent and hearing nuns' confessions!"

Amadeo rolled his eyes.

I thought that Boroni was small-minded, closed in by his clerical life, inexperienced. He had entered the seminary when he was twelve. He was our leader and guide, but he had tasted less of life than most of us.

With the routine, we all began to find a problem in filling our day. We didn't attend university classes, nor did we have homework assignments or term papers to complete. Apart from the conferences, prayer times and meals, we were on our own. Father Boroni's room was across from mine and it was so quiet every afternoon that I believe he was napping. We were young, we didn't want to sleep or study all day, so what was there to do? At this point the practical jokes began.

"Mark, do you remember the zoo?" Amadeo asked just before going to bed one warm night.

"Yes, what about it?" I asked, but he had walked away. The bell rang and the Grand Silence began; after the night prayers we all turned in. I usually read before going to bed but after twenty minutes or so I was tired. I turned off the lights and closed my eyes. I opened them slightly and saw movement in my room: light towards the ceiling. As I rubbed my eyes to focus, I saw fireflies everywhere. I heard some laughter down the corridor but decided not to respond until I had a plan. For the next hour I worked feverishly to shoo the fireflies out my window and leave me in peace.

Luciano was a robust, tall Italian seminarian in our Novice class. Since I had little privacy in my room, having a window on the upstairs walkway, he sometimes stopped by my window to say hello. A few weeks after the firefly incident he walked by and stooped down to pick up a dead baby bird that must have fallen from its nest. Despite my protests he reached over and placed it on my desk. I decided not to react but to exact my revenge. When he returned to his room later that night Lucino found the baby bird on his desk on a plate, with fork, knife and napkin and a glass of wine.

Another afternoon after Boroni had gone to his room, someone found a large cactus leaf and begun throwing it around. I was watching, amused. This went on for about twenty minutes. At three o'clock we were to go to our rooms and there was to be silence until holy hour at seven. When the bell rang to go upstairs Amadeo took the leaf and threw it at me and ran up towards his room. Not to be outdone, I grabbed the prickly thing and chased after him up the stairs and down the corridor. As I passed in front of Boroni's room, cactus in hand, the door swung open and I froze, caught in the act. Boroni angrily scolded us for making noise and ordered us to our rooms. I slunk back.

These kind of things broke up the monotony of daily life in the Novitiate and filled the hours when those of us who were too restless to sleep had nothing to do. There were those who were offended at this behavior, in particular Larry, who was always quick to step out of his room and wag his admonishing finger.

In our group there were Italians, Americans, Canadians and Nigerians. For some reason Father Boroni interacted more with the Canadians, speaking French to them and especially to one named Yves. "Have you noticed how much he likes Yves?" Amadeo asked. "He even likes just saying his name!"

I didn't think much about this until Livinus, a Nigerian, started to have problems with the Novice Master. "No, you cannot go to the doctor; you're like a baby, always complaining!" Boroni told Livinus one day in the corridor. Visibly hurt, Livinus walked by my room quickly, ignoring my invitation to come in and talk.

"Why does he not like me? What have I done to him?" he asked later that evening. "I am having problems with my stomach all the time and I just want to find out what is wrong with me, but he won't let me go to the doctor."

There was preferential treatment going on, and the Nigerians were at the bottom of the ladder. I had never seen racism in action before and was amazed that the priest in charge of our religious formation could be infected by it. I noticed that whenever he looked at Livinus, he frowned and seemed irritated. I learned that many of the Italian seminarians had never met a black man until they entered the seminary. This seemed strange to me, coming as I did from a pluralistic society. Fr. Boroni was not above racism and Livinus was my friend. It wasn't right. I lost respect for the Novice Master. I was worried about Livinus and hoped his health problems were the result of adjusting to Italian food, as Boroni claimed.

Amadeo volunteered to get the garden in order and I offered to help. We began spending more and more time together. Our relationship was one of two buddies who enjoyed each other's company but did not seek out each other exclusively.

"Mark," Amadeo whispered to me one afternoon, "I want to show you something."

When the others had retired, he led me to a secret room high in the tower of one part of the building. I knew there was a hidden chamber below the house; the nuns had hidden Jews there during the Nazi persecution. There was a trapdoor in the middle of the dining room floor covered by a carpet. No one knew about any other hidden spaces, but Amadeo had found that tower room; he spent time up there and invited me to join him. We began to rendezvous there in the afternoons.

One fall day in the secret attic, Amadeo started a playful wrestling match. I had never been much of a fighter and didn't enjoy it even in play. But he was wrestling and I was holding him back. He began to get carried away and became angry and really started to try to hit me, to punch me in the face. With all my might I held him away but he kept going for me, trying to hurt me. I told him to stop and suddenly burst into tears.

It was like Pandora's box as the emotions came flooding out. This was the same as my mysterious silent weeping in college, but no one had ever been such a close witness before. Amadeo's demeanor immediately changed; he seemed at first frightened, then consoling. I sobbed and sobbed as I never had before. When he asked me why I was crying like that, I could only say, "I don't know," and it was true, I didn't know. I only knew that the box that I had tightly closed and pushed to the back of my life was now torn open and its contents were flying out of control.

From that moment on, two things took place: my friendship with Amadeo grew and my need for that friendship became all-consuming. Over the next weeks I began to reveal to Amadeo more of my need and my pain. I was not then aware of its source or cause, but only that it was present and that I could no longer ignore it. During our recreation periods we began to seek each other out, and when we were supposed to be back in our rooms engaged in prayer or study, inevitably we found a way to be together. It was not a sexual relationship, but it was highly emotional. I was completely consumed: the more it gave me, the more I needed it. The dependency became so strong that my ability to look at myself objectively dissipated and my self-esteem sank.

Amadeo suggested one day, "I think we should spend time with other people during our recreation periods." I agreed; it didn't look good for us always to be together. So several weeks later, we tried to fit back into the community. I found myself longing to be with him alone.

One night, after lights out and the Grand Silence, I stole up to Amadeo's room. He had invited me up before the evening prayer. I didn't think about the risk, I was simply overjoyed at the invitation. He asked me to come into his bed, and he held me. I didn't consider this to be a sexual adventure; since early childhood, I had never been held by another human being. I didn't believe it was a sexual experience for him either; it seemed simply an expression of affection. We lay there together and chatted.

It was peaceful until I was shocked out of my skin by a loud knocking on his door. I didn't know what to do. If I was found in his room, in his bed, it would be the end of my life in the seminary. I thought wildly that someone must have seen me go to his room— probably Boroni! Someone must be watching us, looking to see what we were up to. . . .

"Hide under the blanket," he said, before he went to open the door without putting the light on. It turned out that the visitor was Egidio, an Italian seminarian who had a question about the water supply in the house. Amadeo had a brief talk with him before he closed the door and came back to the bed. We were both shaken. "We must never do this again," Amadeo said. "It's too dangerous."

We waited until silence. Then I crept sadly back to my room.

———

Marcus returned. He had considered staying in California to be with his mother and father, but in the end he came back, and was now in the Novitiate. One day in the garden, he said to me, "Mark, if you need anything, let me know. I want to help you if I can."

I asked him what he meant.

"I can see your eyes are red; you've been crying. I know I haven't been a very good friend. But if you ever want to talk about it, I'm here."

I thanked him, but firmly denied that anything was wrong. How could I say anything else? Nothing was really wrong with me at all, except that I needed Amadeo.

During my years at San Vittorino, I had focused on my spiritual life: on prayer, pious reading and developing a relationship with God. I had believed that my human side should be ignored, that it was not to be trusted or listened to. Hadn't even Brother Luigino said as much? The Novitiate was that place set aside in formation in which one is given the opportunity to focus only on this spiritual life. But here my humanity had come to the surface with such force that spirituality played a subservient role. I didn't ask myself how to control it, how to subdue it. Why would I want to subdue it when all I wanted was companionship with this other human being? What's wrong with that, I kept asking myself. Perhaps Amadeo and I will end up together in the same parish, perhaps we can live out our lives together, perhaps this is God's plan for me and I'm just responding to His will. I could almost convince myself of this except for one nagging fact: I had no peace.

It was only many years later that it became clear to me that a boxed-up humanity would be bound to burst open at the most inopportune time. Human emotion is too strong to be pushed aside or imprisoned. I thought about this later period of my life when I read "Little Herr Friedmann" by Thomas Mann, a short story about a well-bred but ugly gentleman whose ordered and seemingly fulfilled life was interrupted by his falling in love with a woman who cared nothing for him. After that he had no peace, and committed suicide because he believed that no one else could satisfy his need to be loved.

This story opened the question for me: the way to peace had to come from something other than suppressing one's humanity. But chasing after every infatuation and emotion could not be the way; the answer could not be either of these two extremes. At that time in the Novitiate, I had no idea of what that answer could be or even how to frame the question. I could only watch as the self-imposed structure, which had kept me safe, crumbled.

As months passed in the Novitiate, I experienced moments of great satisfaction with Amadeo and great unrest in his absence. Spring brought plans to spend three or four weeks in the Italian Alps, in the area of Piedmont not far from Turin. There was a sort of vacation house in the mountains owned by the Oblates and every year the novices and the theology students spent holiday time there. Father Boroni often mentioned this place in his conferences; all year long he seemed to look forward to being there. He told us of the hikes we would take, of the fresh mountain air we would breathe, of the shrines we would visit. But as we prepared for our trip I felt uneasy. On the day of departure I worried: would I have my privacy, my own room? Would I be able to stay close to Amadeo? I feared change, I feared it because I had something I wanted to protect from change.

The drive was long, the tunnels seemed endless. By evening we reached the destination that was unfamiliar to everyone but Boroni. We got out of our van and walked up the path to the residence. The air was cold and crisp, the hills were green and the road was rugged cobblestone. It was a rustic place with a slate roof, dining room barely large enough for all of us, and dorm rooms with two or more beds. When quarters were assigned, I wanted to ask to be with Amadeo, but I didn't dare. I was given a room with two other people. It was a beautiful place, I thought, even though I was tormented by worry about whether I would have time with Amadeo.

After I unpacked and hung up my clothes, I discovered that there were only two bathrooms in the house for thirty of us. I would simply get up early to shower, I said to myself as I turned on the hot water. "SWOOOOOSH!" I jumped back. Next to the sink were large metal canisters with "flammable" written on them; these were attached to a heating system in which visible flames leaped up and enveloped the pipes that guided the water into the sink. Some of the seminarians had complained to Father Boroni and to another priest in charge, Father Manone, about the possible dangers of this system. The response came in unison: "You rich Americans! You're always used to your luxuries! Try to rough it for once!"

It soon became clear that Father Boroni's love of hiking went beyond passion to obsession. He took all of us up steep, rock-hewed mountains, by no means easy climbs. He started us with two-hour walks, then three, then up to five hours.

Most of us didn't enjoy it at all since he hurried us and didn't pace himself for a large group. He often disappeared up the mountain leaving us behind trying to catch up. One day he let us vote on whether to take an all-day trek or go to Pinerollo, a town near Turin. Somehow he was able to sway the vote towards the hike, so hike we did.

It was the most difficult climb we had ever done, scrambling over boulders, balancing on precipitous paths and pulling one another up over steep slopes. About halfway up, Luciano, the sturdily built Italian from Milan, began to groan loudly, "Oh, Pinerollo!!" About three hours into our climb a Canadian tripped, fell and sprained his ankle. He couldn't walk. But Father Boroni went on, saying we must reach the top, so we had to carry this person all the way up and all the way down. After this experience we all hated the hikes.

When we didn't go hiking, we took day trips in the area. In Turin we visited a hospital that had been run by St. John Bosco, various churches containing the tombs of saints, and the cathedral where the Shroud is kept. I wasn't much interested in the saints from Turin, but I had read a lot about the Shroud of Turin and was looking forward to that experience. I found the cathedral of the Shroud disappointing; it seemed oppressive, with walls and floor of dark marble. The Shroud cannot be viewed; it is wrapped up and kept in a box in a special chapel to safeguard it against damage from light and humidity. We were led into the sacristy to view a life-sized photograph of it but it was the Shroud itself that interested me, and not still another photograph of it.

I had read that Turin had a respectable Egyptian museum. As we got back into the van, I asked Father Boroni in a loud voice so all could hear, "Can we go to the Egyptian museum?" I had always enjoyed visiting European churches and shrines, but they were all starting to look alike, and I wanted to do something culturally different. "Baruffo!" he responded, "Clown!" Everyone looked at me as if I was from Mars. Apparently doing anything non-religious was perceived as inappropriate and my suggestion was taken as a joke.

Other day-trips took us to various Marian shrines in the Alps; one very large one was Our Lady of Europa, nestled in the mountains, but with a church almost the size of St. Peter's in Rome. It had been built to enshrine the black Madonna, said to be a miraculous image carved from dark stone; it looked like a woman and child trapped inside a cocoon.

"Why are the miraculous images of the Madonna always the ugly ones?" Francis, an American, whispered in my ear.

I had heard this comment time and time again and I couldn't help laughing; it was so true. Why couldn't miracles happen through a Raphael or a Botticelli, I wondered. Apart from the Cocoon Madonna itself, the shrine's design and its capacity to hold tens of thousands of pilgrims in its isolated, remote location, was impressive. I had never seen anything like it in America.

On other days we visited other shrines, all dedicated to the Madonna. Each had its story of miraculous origins, usually stemming from an apparition or a painting by Saint Luke. As we drove away from one of these churches, I blurted, "The Madonna must not like heaven very much." Everyone turned and stared at me. "She's always in Italy!" I said. The Americans laughed, the Italians gasped. I fed on the gasp: "If it's true that she has appeared in Italy all these times, how do you explain the fact that she hasn't appeared on every mountaintop in the United States?"

"Because you don't have faith," was the answer from the Italians, practically in unison. I decided to let it go. Certainly it was possible that the Madonna had appeared at various times and in various places, but I had a hard time believing that she had appeared on every Italian hilltop.

The next day we set out for Loreto, a town with a large cathedral built around a house. The small house inside the cathedral is said to be from Ephesus, the house in which the

Virgin Mary lived. We were told that it had been miraculously transported to Loreto, I had never heard of this shrine before. When we arrived, it was clear that Loreto itself existed for pilgrimages; there were an endless variety of vendors of religious articles on the long hill to the shrine. Inside the church, right in the middle under the dome, was a little building, covered inside and out with decorative marble. The guide explained that under the marble, the house was made of stones native to Ephesus, which gave great credibility to the story of its origin. Angels, he said, carried the house to Loreto and set it down on this spot.

"Sounds like the *Wizard of Oz* to me," Francis whispered in my ear.

It was more difficult for the Americans to believe these things than it was for the Italians. Perhaps this was a cultural difference that I didn't understand. Americans, it seemed, relied on rationality as a measure of what to accept, while Italians were influenced by aesthetics. For Americans to believe something, it had to be reasonable; for the Italians, if it was beautiful and wonderful it had to be true. Eventually I came to value their viewpoint instead of scoffing at it.

"Mail call!" rang out the next morning. I had received no letters for the several months I had been at the Novitiate, and this was the first time the mail had been brought up from Rome. I was surprised to find a letter from my father. I opened it quickly. He was writing to tell me that our dog Cindy had died two months earlier. I had grown up with that dog and loved her. I hadn't even known she was ill. I felt anger: why couldn't he have called me when she died? Why wait two months to inform me? I never want to go back there again, I thought. I was too angry to mourn Cindy. The seminary, for better or worse, was my home; there was no other place for me.

Amadeo and I found a field next to the house where we could meet and talk in the evenings. Privacy was hard to find. Though I valued the opportunity to be with him, I found it difficult since we now had so little time together. My emotional needs were like a car sputtering for gas and receiving only a drop or two occasionally, just enough to keep it sputtering. Need overwhelmed me and continued to burrow into my self-esteem. I felt inadequate and stupid. Any of my talents or strengths were buried and consumed by my need for someone else. I found myself longing to be back in Rome in the Novitiate house, to the predictable life we had had before we left on this trip. But I knew everything would be different when we returned: a week-long retreat and then the final preparations for the vows of poverty, chastity and obedience. Our lives would belong more and more to the Oblates of the Virgin Mary and no longer to ourselves. This frightened me and I tried not to think about it.

The cycle of hiking and visiting shrines continued for several weeks until the day when we packed our bags and closed up the house. As I looked back at the mountains, clear and crisp blue in the morning air, I wondered if I would ever return here. These weeks had been difficult for me and I was grateful to return to Rome. At the same time, I was afraid of what the future might bring, and, struggling to see my life in the light of faith, asked God to guide my steps and help me finally find peace.

———

Father Basil, a tall, bald Oblate priest from India who worked at the Vatican, had agreed to take care of the Novitiate house for the weeks we were away.

"The garden died," Basil told Amadeo dryly on our arrival.

"Died!" Amadeo exclaimed afterwards. "More like 'I didn't water while you were away!'" We had worked hard, planting rows of flowers and vegetables. Now it was all dried up. Notwithstanding this setback, I was glad to be back in my private room, safe in the Novitiate routine. Even though it would not last long, I relished those few days.

The taking of the vows of poverty, chastity and obedience was our Profession; this would take place at San Vittorino in five weeks. After that we were permitted to go home for about forty days. Amadeo asked me to come stay with him after the Profession.

I would love to, but I'm going home to California the day after. I already have my ticket."

"Why don't you come back to Italy early, come stay at my house for a week, then we can go down to Rome together?"

I agreed; I found the prospect exciting.

"But," he added, "don't tell anyone. Okay?"

I didn't understand why it mattered if others knew or not, but I agreed to the secrecy, and so plans were made. From then on, Amadeo would often tell me dreamily about his town high in the Italian Dolomites, and the people who were part of his life there.

The retreat to prepare for our Profession began and so did a week of silence. I felt fairly peaceful during that week and enjoyed the conferences by a new Oblate priest who was from the island of Pantelleria. He was highly educated, experienced, rotund and funny. At a break during one of his conferences he described a Sicilian cheese which is full of white worms and how he loved to pick out the worms and eat them one by one. He was not always joking, however. His talks consisted of reflections on the writings of Father Lanteri, the Oblate founder. Some of the writings were purely a reflection of their time, he explained one day, and should not be taken literally. Lanteri, wrote, for example, that one should never wrinkle one's forehead, for that would show a lack of patience. Many passages seemed extremely rigid. Mostly Lanteri's directives had to do with the spiritual life, but I had noticed a passage in which he warned against "particular friendships."

What did that mean, I wondered, is he saying one should have no friends? I once unkindly told Amadeo: "Larry probably tells himself he's following the rule better than anyone else, since he has no friends!" Amadeo and I seemed to be in clear violation of this precept. So I asked the padre giving us the conferences if he could clarify what Lanteri was saying. I was told, "He is simply warning against homosexuality." I was a bit shocked. But I thought that since my friendship with Amadeo had nothing to do with homosexuality, it wouldn't be in violation of the rule. I could set my mind at rest; I didn't have to think about this any more.

The day of the Profession drew near. It seemed to become real one day when the tailor came to measure us for our religious habit: a long black robe or cassock with a thick sash around the waist and a Roman collar. Things seemed suddenly to be accelerating and I began to feel off-balance. I wanted to make the Profession but felt unsure. I was promising God that I would always be chaste, always be poor and always obedient, but would I keep these promises? Could I trust myself? Am I ready? Even though the vows were for only one year, to be renewed annually for three years until the final vows, it still felt like forever. "Trust in God; he will do the rest," Father Boroni told us. So, as if I were taking a leap into a pool and hoping not to drown, I decided to take that step. After all, where else would I go?

Brother Luigino had become a distant figure; he had not been much involved in our life at the Novitiate. The Profession ceremony was in the turbine shrine at San Vittorino; Luigino was present as well as the Rector Major who was the head of the Oblates. I couldn't appreciate the beauty of the ceremony itself because I wept the entire time. I did not know why I was crying; it was not out of happiness but it was not from sadness either. It was from a fear of this new life, a feeling of my own inadequacy and of the pain and need that had consumed me over the past year. As I pronounced the three vows of poverty, chastity and obedience, I felt as if I were stepping off a cliff, hoping there would be a net. I looked around at those who had gone before: the priests, nuns, Brother Luigino, other religious and wondered how my life would be, how it would turn out, whether I would live those words which I pronounced. It was a leap of faith filled with fear.

There was a buffet lunch after the ceremony. Some of the families of the Italians were there. As I stood eating my *panino*, I felt that I had arrived at an important point in my life. I would be different, more focused on my relationship with God, who would help me to grow and find peace. Looking around, there was a sea of black: the religious garb was to be the outward sign that we were now consecrated to God; we were to wear the black robe as much as possible. Since the Profession was in September and school began in mid-October, we had all made plans to go home and visit our families. It was to be our last scheduled visit for three years. It was expected that we would grow away from our homes, from our families and those places we were from and would become more and more part of this new "Oblate family." I was eager to return to the U.S., but did feel a bit awkward traveling in the religious habit and wearing it at home. Still, I wanted to follow all the rules, to be as faithful as possible to this new life. So I put on my black robe the next morning and took the bus to the airport in Rome.

I called my father from New York to tell him I would be arriving in San Francisco that evening. He said that they couldn't pick me up because they were going to the opera. "Take a bus to Modesto," he said, "and I'll pick you up there. I have the bus schedule here for you."

"Okay," I said, as my heart sank.

I was always excited about going home, building up the image of my life in California during the year, missing it, longing for it. But when I was finally there, reality struck and I could never understand why I had been looking forward to returning. I was already tired from my flight, and dreaded arriving in San Francisco and getting to the bus depot, which was far from the airport.

I wondered how my father would react when he saw me in my habit for the first time. He had never acknowledged my being in the seminary or studying for the priesthood. It seemed it was an embarrassing topic at home. Would this change everything? Absorbed in these thoughts, I got off the bus, exhausted; it was late at night in Modesto. It had been an ordeal finding the bus in San Francisco after being on the plane so long, and another ordeal going to the depot in that terrible section of Modesto.

"Mark!" my father called and held out his hand for a hand-shake. "How are you?"

"Tired," I replied. He said nothing about my cassock; it was as if it was invisible. I thought when I arrived that every-one was indifferent to me: I was dressed all in black in this habit with a roman collar, and no one at home seemed even to notice. I wondered why that was. It seemed someone would be interested enough to ask why I was wearing that robe. And then I would explain. No one, I thought, was interested in my life. I would simply wait out the month or so until I could go back to Italy and visit Amadeo, who was interested in me, and his family.

But I see now that what I took to be indifference probably reflected fear: I was afraid of being rejected if I shared my com-mitment to the religious life, and I did not realize that others too might be afraid, not knowing how to relate to something so alien to their experience. Those who profess a strong com-mitment to an ideal, whether it be faith or a different way of life, are often feared by those closest to them. When does com-mitment become fanaticism? When does a strong belief seem to others like intolerance? It was these unanswered questions that clouded those days, but neither I nor my family knew how to deal with them.

Longing Becomes Unhappiness

———

BEFORE I RETURNED TO ITALY IN 1981, news reached me of the death of Sean, the cleric from Dublin who had helped me through my first philosophy exams.

"Did you hear how he died?" I asked Marcus on the phone.

"He died in the Oblate vacation house we just left. I heard he died in the bathroom, taking a bath. He was poisoned by the gas leaking out of one of those tanks under the sink that heat the water. Remember we complained about how dangerous those tanks were?"

I did remember, and I remembered too that the response was an accusation aimed at the Americans. I felt angry that Father Boroni and another Italian priest, Father Manone, had taken that hostile attitude when the matter had been brought to their attention. I wondered how the others would feel about it. I told myself that I would deal with Sean's death once I got back to Rome.

"Marcus," I said, "I'm going back to Europe early to travel for a week or two. So I'll see you in Rome."

"Where are you going?"

"Northern Italy," I responded, vaguely. Marcus was too inquisitive.

———

The air felt crisp enough to crack as I stepped onto the train platform in Amadeo's village. The Dolomites, craggy mountain peaks, were covered with snow, the slopes that the village was built on were verdant green and the sky was the bluest I had ever seen. I looked around the platform and saw no one whom I knew. Then I heard: "Marco!" as Amadeo appeared and grabbed my suitcase. I was happy to be there; I felt wanted. I had felt that so rarely in the past that I reveled in it here.

His family's house was modest, consisting of a main room or kitchen, one bathroom and several small bedrooms, all on different levels. There was no living room or family room, just a sofa and a table in the kitchen. The house was freezing, at least to me, having just come from California.

"You rest," Amadeo said as he showed me to my room. I slept until time for the midday meal, or *pranzo*. His mother had prepared a feast: large ravioli with butter sauce, wild mushrooms, veal, lettuce and wine. I was glad to be here, especially because I was with Amadeo. I hoped that my visit would cement our friendship.

He was proud of his home and of his village. He had two brothers and one sister: the eldest brother, who worked in hotel management, took an immediate liking to me, and I liked him too. He was effeminate, and I thought he was probably homosexual. The other brother and sister were still in the rebellious stage, in their late teens; neither worked but both were friendly. I felt a bond with them that I hoped would grow. Amadeo introduced me to his parish priest, a large gray-haired man with a piercing stare and a quick smile. Amadeo had always wanted to be like him. In the next days I met his other friends, all older women. I didn't ask him why he didn't seem to have any male friends of his own age. I didn't want to risk hurting his feelings.

Amadeo had always wanted to be a cleric; as a child he had played he was a priest, giving his little brother and sister bread for communion, baptizing their pets and hearing their confessions. His father was dead, so the parish priest became a father figure for him. He had a strong work ethic from his mother who cleaned a school every afternoon. He was an easy person to spend time with; he liked to tell long, detailed stories about his childhood, his family and his village. In Rome he had gotten along with everybody except the seminarians from southern Italy, especially Naples, whom he considered stupid and lacking commonsense.

Those were gentle and relaxing days; the pain and need I had felt in Rome subsided. Was this the beginning of a peaceful and happy year? I hoped so. The days passed quickly and soon it was time to return to the seminary. Amadeo suggested that I take the train to Rome the next day. He would leave the day after that, so no one would ever guess that I had been in his village.

I agreed and left, with much hugging and many promises to return. But I never saw his family again.

In Rome, we were now assigned to live at St. Elena, the clerics' house. Marcus had already been there for two days when I saw him in the dining room. "We thought you got lost in Europe," he said.

"No," I told him, "I was just traveling around."

I thought he was being rather inquisitive, so I changed the subject, and Marcus proceeded to show me around. The house had been built next to the parish church of Saint Helen's, near the Basilica of St. John Lateran. The parish was in a lower-class neighborhood on Via Casilina, filled with dilapidated apartment buildings. There was no foliage or trees anywhere, only cement and asphalt. Our house was across the street from the railroad tracks and every fifteen minutes or so, the whole building shook as if there were an earthquake. "It rumbles like that day and night but they say you get used to it," Marcus said. Next to us was the only playground in that neighborhood. With the shaking and the kids screaming, it was hardly a tranquil environment.

That night I looked out the window, searching for the stars. But because of air pollution and the city lights, I couldn't see any. They've taken away my stars, I said to myself as I closed the curtains. I felt as if I were a boat bobbing on the water, hoping to keep afloat but not knowing how.

The next morning Amadeo arrived. We greeted each other casually although I really did not understand why we had to keep our friendship secret.

We had not yet been assigned permanent rooms. Father Manone, a pale, dark-haired, rather effeminate man, announced at lunch that there were not enough single rooms for everyone; some of us would have to have roommates. He seemed to lack self confidence, chuckling frequently to mask his discomfort. We had a meeting that evening to decide on the room situation. Space was so tight at St. Elena that the conference room was in a small chapel on the second floor with fluorescent lighting and hard seats. The room was so crowded that some of us had to stand in back.

"Are there any of you who want to volunteer to be roommates?" Manone asked.

To my surprise, Amadeo raised his hand. "Yves and I volunteer."

Yves was the French Canadian in my Novitiate class who had been the favorite of Father Boroni. He was an intelligent and likable person. Amadeo had not discussed this decision with me.

I was given a room facing the railroad tracks, with my own private bathroom. I felt like a king. Yves and Amadeo were two doors down, but Amadeo seemed an eternity away. Over the next days, weeks, and months I came to see that he was pulling away from me and was more and more focused on Yves. In a short time they became inseparable and very happy to be sharing quarters. I really couldn't dislike Yves because he was such a vibrant and considerate person that I had to respect him. Amadeo was still friendly, but our special relationship had ended. To be able to talk to him, I had to knock at his door and ask him to stop by my room. It was becoming awkward and I was lonely. I told Maurizio, who had become the house medic, that I was feeling a little down lately, physically and emotionally. "Do you have some vitamins or something you can give me to help?" I asked him. "And can you keep this between ourselves?"

He said he did have something, and that I would feel better after I took it for two weeks. He gave me tiny bottles of some sort of vitamin-and-mineral elixir, but it didn't make me feel any better. I couldn't understand why I was so miserable, when I knew I was where God wanted me to be. I spoke with no one about this. How could I? I didn't know how to talk about my feelings. And anyway, I was supposed to ignore them.

———

"I hate him," Dave said to me one day. He was talking about Father Manone. "We told him how dangerous those gas tanks were, even Sean told him! I hate him because Sean is dead because of him." The next afternoon Dave asked me, "Did you hear what is going on in Pinerolo this week? They're demolishing the summer house. Right now it's a pile of rubble. That's how they're making sure there won't be a lawsuit or any investigation."

It was true. The vacation house had been torn down without any explanation. All the Americans who were in Sean's class blamed Manone for Sean's death. Manone seemed intimated by the Americans; he tried to avoid them. But he was in charge of all the clerics in the house; he was their point of reference. I found myself taking a strong dislike to Manone. He struck me as deceitful, ill-intentioned and weak-spirited.

A small group of Americans who had been especially close to Sean more than blamed Manone; they loathed him. They were treated like the black sheep of the community because they were cynical and bitter. I found their company refreshing and spent more and more time with them. They seemed to have more empathy than the others. The other Americans in my class wanted to please Father Manone and the Italian superiors. That was what we had been taught, after all. Brother Luigino had taught us that to do God's will was to do the will of our superior. I found this precept more and more distasteful; it seemed to me to be a way to quash discussion and questioning.

It was in this atmosphere that we began our theological studies at the Angelicum. There were two sections: English and Italian. In first-year theology, there were two famous professors in the Italian section; everyone was trying to get into their classes. Since I knew Italian, I thought I would take some courses in Italian and some in English, but there were too many conflicts. I decided to take all my classes in the Italian section the first year and in the English section the second year, so that I could get the benefit of the prominent professors and I could also share classes with Amadeo.

When we got back to St. Elena after the first day of classes, Marcus asked me how things had gone. I told him it was okay, but that we had one professor who asked where everyone was from—who was from France, who was from Italy, who was from Spain. When he asked who was from the United States, a few people raised their hands. Then he asked who was from California.

Marcus agreed that it was strange that California should be seen as a separate entity from the rest of the States. But there actually was a difference between the seminarians from California and those from other parts of the U.S. The Californians tended to be less formal socially and less rigid about religion. And they often came from relatively unconventional backgrounds, while the other Americans had grown up in large, staunchly Catholic families.

There were lectures five days a week, four hours a day and a two-hour class in Spiritual Theology on Friday afternoons.

Latin classes were held on Tuesday and Thursday afternoons. I enjoyed some of my courses and found dogmatic theology fascinating. Dogmatic theology is that branch which utilizes philosophy as its instrument in investigating such mysteries as Who is Christ? (Christology); the nature of God, the nature of the Trinity, etc. But I didn't like all my courses; I really hated Scripture classes.

I complained about them to Dave one day at lunch. "The whole science of Biblical studies is a house of cards! In five or ten years, the theories will change and what we are learning now will be thrown out. Plus, they don't lead us through any reasoning. The professors say things like '*All* the experts today hold that the Gospel of John was written after the year 150 A.D.,' or '*Everyone today* holds that Moses had nothing to do with writing any books of the Bible.' That's no way to teach. Tell me why they hold such things to be true and let me decide if I buy it or not. Basically he's saying that if we don't accept these theories, something is wrong with us."

Dave nodded; he didn't seem particularly interested.

Throwing myself into my studies gave my life some focus. I wanted to learn how to conquer my emotions, and maybe this was the way. I spent hours in the library doing extra reading and research. I found most of theology fascinating and applied myself with rigor to the writings of Augustine and Aquinas. I began to take forty-five minutes to walk to the university, giving myself time to wake up before classes began and also to think about my situation. I did this for some two years.

One day I asked Amadeo if he wanted to walk to school with me. "No," he said, "I get too sweaty and worked up when I walk." At school, he was always with Yves. I told myself that was okay; focusing on my studies made me feel more stable. The magic of the first years at San Vittorino dissipated while I was at St. Elena. Despite my focus on academics, as the months passed I became once again weak and needy, struggling with my attachment to Amadeo. I kept trying to spend time with

him, grateful for even a ten-minute visit. Then my heart would
plunge into sadness. It got to the point that I actually felt physical pain in my chest. Could my suffering heart manifest itself
in my body? If only I could escape this attachment, this need
for him! I had to find a way to deaden my feelings completely;
obviously concentrating on my studies wasn't enough. I felt
trapped.

At least when I had been back in California, even for that
last short visit, he had faded from my consciousness. But I
couldn't return home for another three years. I was absorbed
in these thoughts while I was walking on the upper terrace and
glancing down, I spotted Amadeo. I felt my heart move, jerk; it
was a kind of fear that enveloped me, a fear of being quashed,
crushed by this attachment. I couldn't seem to get over it, I
couldn't rise above it, I couldn't deaden it. Ensnared, I began
desperately to think of a way out, a way to find peace.

I told Marcus in confidence one evening that I was going to
ask to go home that summer. "I'm so exhausted that I need to
go home and rest," I said. "I need to get away."

I was shocked when he replied, "I already spoke to Father
Manone, and *I'm* going home to be with my family."

That was all the push I needed to ask to return home too,
but I knew that Manone would never allow it. I decided to go
over his head, to his superior, Father Bergamo, who, in addition to being the head of the community, was the pastor of the
parish and seemed more reasonable. A few days later I found
myself in his office. "I'm exhausted and I need to go home for
a few months. Can I borrow the money and pay you back?"

He was surprisingly agreeable and told me I could leave right
after my exams. I decided not to say anything to Amadeo. I
had to get away from him, to close my heart to him. I arranged
to leave early in the morning and slip out to the airport unno-
ticed. As I prepared to leave; I felt newly hopeful that I would
find the road to happiness.

One Journey Ends

———

It WAS 1982. I HAD BEEN away from the U.S. for five years. Each time I returned, American society, infused with pop culture, seemed ever more alien to me. I felt as if I was from Mars. I found computer games dull, popular songs insipid, and vernacular juvenile. The whole country seemed to be immersed in superficial, meaningless trends. I was the outsider. I didn't want to become part of this world in which I now found myself, but I had to function in it. Both my parents were working and our strained relationships recurred. But I was home for a purpose: to forget about Amadeo, to rest and return to Rome a new person in the fall.

I soon established a daily routine that suited me: I spent my days alone along the river, taking walks, watching the water and the people, sometimes reading, and listening to the sounds of the birds. Being alone seemed the only way I could find some peace. My days were certainly not full, but I did have a sort of schedule. I found myself longing to share my time with another but that was not possible, for there was no other.

I stayed with my grandmother and had little contact with the rest of my family. I was the only sibling left in Modesto; the others had moved away. I was broke and had to earn some money. A wealthy family hired me to do some gardening; every day I shoveled dirt, preparing soil for planting, and eventually I did landscaping for a small shopping mall. I was glad to have this job, not only because it would pay enough for another plane ticket, but because it allowed me time both to think and to create something beautiful.

I didn't heard from Marcus for several weeks, but one day he called me, obviously upset. "Mark," he said, "Livinus died! I just got a call from Italy." Livinus was that sweet Nigerian man who had been a part of my life since the first week I arrived in San Vittorino. He always thought of others and always had a bright smile. I was shocked.

"They think it was a heart attack," Marcus said. "They were playing soccer, and he just sat down on the field and died. He was thirty-three years old, just like Sean. I wonder if that's an omen."

There was silence on the phone for a moment. Then I said that this made me really angry at Father Boroni; "Livinus was always complaining about not feeling well, but Boroni wouldn't let him go to a doctor."

Livinus was gone. Sean was dead. Did those Italian superiors really care about us foreigners at all? Two deaths in two years, both preventable. I now understood even more clearly the bitterness of those who blamed Father Manone for Sean's death.

Those summer days passed quickly and I soon had to make arrangements to return to Rome. I really had not resolved anything; I still felt unsure and unhappy, but I couldn't think of any alternative, I knew of no other way to move forward in my life. Amadeo had faded from my mind; I could count that as one accomplishment. If I could keep my heart away from him, perhaps my future would be more peaceful. With these thoughts I boarded the plane from San Francisco and landed in Italy the next morning.

––––

"Damn you, how did you get to go home?" Steve demanded angrily in the courtyard at St. Elena's after dinner the day I arrived. I mumbled an answer as I spied Amadeo in the distance. I wouldn't go up to him; I intended to have a distant and casual relationship with him from then on. I realized when I saw him that the visit home had done me good: my feelings toward him had dried up. In the days that followed I found myself able to deal with him as a friend, albeit distant, without aching inside. My time in California was a success; it had enabled me to gather up my emotions, pack them neatly away, and move forward. Of course I would have to watch myself, to be careful, not to allow my needs to consume me again. I would watch my every step. It was the beginning of my fifth year in Rome and I felt that I could refocus myself on my spiritual life and my studies, and in that way I could be content.

Other friendships blossomed for me during that year, particularly with Patrick, whom I had known from college in California, where he was one year behind me. He was from upstate New York and had a riotous sense of humor coupled with a positive spirit. He was a joy to be with and he liked my company as well. I also spent more and more time with Dave and Tom, sharing their bitterness towards the Italian superiors over the deaths of Livinus and Sean. Whenever Father Manone looked into the TV room and spied the "black sheep," he left hastily, obviously feeling threatened. I knew that my friendship with them would mark me as a rebel. But that didn't matter. I liked Dave and Tom; they had been Sean's closest friends. I began to feel part of the community. I could enjoy my friends without feeling dependent or emotionally torn.

"Tomorrow we will hold Livinus's funeral," Father Manone announced at lunch the next day. "The body will be brought here tomorrow morning and afterward it will be sent to his family in Nigeria for burial."

Livinus had been dead for over a month, and I did not look forward to facing the reality of his death at the funeral. The next day, as I walked into the church, the first thing I noticed was the worst stench I had smelled in my life coming from the metallic coffin.

Apparently, the body had not been embalmed or refrigerated, but had been kept in a morgue. The Italian superiors had sent word to the family that it would be too costly to send it to Nigeria. The Nigerian community in Rome had organized to raise the money to send Livinus home. Hence, the delay in the funeral.

During the service the only emotion I felt was anger. I tried to mourn Livinus, but my irritation was too great. Every few minutes during the Mass, one of the Nigerian representatives sprayed air freshener around the casket while Father Manone nodded approvingly.

What is going on here? I asked myself. The Oblates had plenty of money; they could have sent Livinus home if they chose to. It's just not important to them, I thought. The Oblate order owned a large successful department store in Pisa, and donations coming into San Vittorino amounted to millions of dollars. Was this all we were to the Oblates: bodies to be disposed of when they were no longer useful? What about the family of Livinus or Sean or any of us? Were any of us safe in this environment? Were our lives and well-being worth anything to the heads of the Oblates? Deep resentment festered towards Manone and the other Italian superiors.

———

When school began, routine set in. I was now free of Amadeo, liberated from those oppressive feelings that had enslaved me. I thought I could finally be at peace. I enjoyed my companions and relished recreation time when we could chat, stroll or play board games. "You guys should keep it down in here," Larry admonished, sticking his head into the room where a few of us were playing a loud card game.

When he left, I rolled my eyes. "I'm scared of him," I said. "He's so uptight! Some night I'm going to wake up in the middle of the night and find Larry standing over me, naked, with a knife in his hand, ready to plunge it in."

Everyone roared with laughter, but when I got to my room that night, I really did feel frightened enough to lock my door.

Although I was warming up to the community, I often felt an inexplicable sadness. It was as if my attachment to Amadeo had dug a space which now had to be filled; before my friendship with him that space either had not been there or was buried so deep I was unaware of it. Once more I began to walk to school in the mornings, through the dilapidated neighborhood, under the ancient Porta Maggiore, cutting through the basilica of St. John Lateran and on down to the Angelicum.

On the way to school one morning in February, I found myself particularly depressed. Why was that? Here I was doing God's will in Rome, following the road to the priesthood, applying myself to my studies and to the seminary life, obeying all the regulations. And still I was unhappy. It didn't make sense. I felt so miserable that day that tears rolled down my face as I walked.

People will see you, Mark, get it together! I told myself. You're in a cassock, you're committed to God; you should be happy. People can't see you looking sad when you're dressed like this. But wait, I thought, if God doesn't send me happiness when I'm doing His will, then what do I care if people see me crying when I'm dressed as a priest?

It had never occurred to me that God could be speaking to me through my sorrow, that His will that I tried to obey could be revealed, not by Brother Luigino or the directives of the religious superiors, but in my heart, which could sense what was right and what was wrong for me before my mind could grasp it. But I didn't trust myself; these were just feelings, I told myself. It would take years for my intellect to learn to tune in to my heart.

We were required to meet with Father Manone to open ourselves up and seek his guidance. This was the monthly meeting with the superior prescribed by the rule of the Order. I didn't trust Manone and wasn't going to tell him what I was going through. Most of us kept our appointments with him mainly so that we could get our ten-dollar-per-month stipend. I kept my assigned meetings during the first eight months that year, even though it was obvious that Manone didn't like me. I wasn't sure why; I thought he probably disliked the Americans in general.

My very last meeting with him was on a winter afternoon. I usually talked to him about my studies, assuring him that everything was going great and that I was completely happy and contented. As a rule, he didn't say much in response, until that afternoon.

"I have a few things to say," he began, as he sat behind his desk, his round pale face gazing back at me like a large insipid moon. "There is an odor coming from you which is offensive. It smells almost medicinal. Probably others are shy about telling you. I have noticed it several times when I walk by. I wanted to make you aware of this."

Of course I was embarrassed and offended. "I was sick for awhile; maybe it's the medicine," I said. "I shower every day, sometimes twice a day." I added that I would get my cassock dry-cleaned. I didn't mention that I had just had it cleaned. I wondered if he was telling me this just to hurt me.

"Another thing I have noticed," he continued, "is the way that you look at others. I have noticed your look. It shows something about you, something that one day might lead to, I don't know, homosexuality." He looked down, frowning, avoiding my eyes.

I was flabbergasted at the accusation. What could he mean by "looking at others"? Was he accusing me of being homosexual? Was I homosexual? Why was he bringing this up? I tried to look calm, thanked him for his time and walked out.

I stink and he thinks I'm gay, I thought.

I had come here to dedicate my life to God and couldn't think of myself in contradiction to that dedication. At that time I was struggling with my self-esteem, seeking from others, especially Amadeo, a sense of my own worth. Validation is what I craved, since I didn't know or love myself. Being homosexual, I thought, would be in contradiction to my commitment to Christ. I knew that I had some sexual feelings towards men, but I reasoned that this was simply due to my all-male environment and to certain factors in my upbringing. It was a temporary situation, in other words. And since sexuality had no place in the life of a cleric, I wouldn't have to focus on it. Whatever my sexuality was, it needed to be pushed aside. Manone was bringing this up to wound me, that was all.

I happened to come across Dave in the corridor. I told him that I hated meeting with Manone and asked him whether he still kept his appointments with him. "I haven't met with him since last year," Dave said. "For the ten dollars, just ask him when he's not in his room—the best place is on the stairs. He'll hand it to you and then you don't have to meet with him."

I took Dave's advice and put the monthly meetings with Manone behind me. I didn't feel that he had my best interests at heart and I didn't trust him or anything he said. But the next day I brought my cassock to the dry cleaners.

One evening the head of the Oblates, called the Rector Major, came to the seminary to hold a conference for us theology students. He seemed a distant figure, not very personable, and had no rapport at all with the American priests or seminarians. There had been a discussion in the seminary recently about where the newly ordained priests would be sent, since there was only one Oblate house in the United States. The Rector Major came to clarify that point.

"The road to sanctity is obedience to the will of God," he began, in the fluorescent-lit chapel/conference room. "It is obedience to His will not as I imagine it, but as manifested in the Church. Within the religious life His will is shown to me by the superiors. It is by adhering to what I am asked to do that I can be assured that I am following His will for me . . ."

I leaned over to Dave and whispered, "So he's saying that he's God's voice for us, then? Right?" Dave nodded, frowning. I was irritated at the thrust of this message. What was he trying to impose on us?

The Rector Major continued. "Our congregation plans a great expansion in South America, especially in Argentina. Most of the newly ordained will be sent to South America. This is our mission. The Church in South America is in great need and awaits our help . . ."

I was dejected after the conference. I had always imagined that I would end up back in the United States. I hadn't even thought of the possibility of being sent to another country for the rest of my life. The Rector Major's presentation of the question prevented discussion of its wisdom. He was the boss; he was God's will.

I had a growing feeling of being trapped. Since each of us had to have a priest as our spiritual director, I chose one from outside the Oblates, a Jesuit from Los Angeles who lived near the Vatican. I could confide my thoughts and feelings to him without fear of repercussions. After I had been seeing him for several months, he said, "It seems you feel like a log in a mill, moving towards the saw without any say-so or control." He was perceptive and put into words feelings that I didn't dare express to myself. That conversation with him was the beginning of my desire to leave the sawmill. These were new and frightening feelings of wanting to escape, to put the whole Oblate experience behind me.

Months passed. I took extra classes at school requiring me to stay at the university until evening. I was busy, but my mind felt clouded. I was going through the motions of seminary life, but all desires faded as one greater yearning grew: to leave this place, to seek a new existence. My whole life was cast into more and more uncertainty and my greatest and eventually my *only* certainty became my desire to leave. I *had* to depart, to return to California. I didn't know how I had reached that point of desperation, but I knew that if I didn't leave, I would self-destruct emotionally or physically. I would fall apart. I would be deeply unhappy.

I had saved up about two dollars of phone tokens, enough to make about a thirty-second phone call to the United States. My heart raced as I reached a daring decision. I left a message on my father's answering machine, telling him to call me. Hours passed and no phone call, but during dinner the announcement came: "Mark Tedesco, telephone." As I got up, the Italians sitting near me said, "What's this about? Tedesco never gets phone calls!" I ran upstairs to the most isolated part of the house.

"Dad, I want to come home. Is that okay with you?"

He replied at once: "Yes, Mark, come."

"I want to go to the university when I get home. Can you get me the information to enroll at Berkeley along with the application forms? Can you get them ready for me?"

He reassured me that he would, and he would help me with the airfare, if necessary. I couldn't believe it; I was actually taking steps to leave. Now that my father had agreed, all I needed to do was arrange things on my side.

Leaving the seminary was like leaving a marriage; it's a relationship that becomes a part of one's life. I wanted to leave; at the same time I wanted to remain tied to my life here, my history, my friends and the road to the priesthood. But I had to leave because I was so unhappy and because I didn't know if I wanted to be a permanent member of the Oblates. How could I have both? I decided to ask for a one-year leave of absence. I would talk directly with Father Bergamo, the pastor, bypassing Manone again. And I would go to Brother Luigino and speak with him about it.

"I thought you came back too soon, so I'm not surprised you're asking for more time off," Father Bergamo said. He made it so easy. I implored him not to tell anyone in the community. A few days later I took the bus to see Brother Luigino. Although he had become a distant figure to me, he was still *Il Santo* and I wanted to get his permission. I met with him in his room, but now his attitude toward me was different from the other times I had been with him. Now he treated me as an equal. No embraces, only conversation. I told him that I needed to be certain before ordination and this time off would help me to gain that certainty, that I was becoming more and more confused the longer I stayed at St. Elena's. He agreed that this was a prudent choice, making me feel even more justified and determined. But if he had objected, I would still have remained resolute, things having gone this far.

I took the bus back to Rome, feeling both frightened and excited. My whole life was about to change again. The future was uncertain, but this uncertainty was more appealing than the certainty of remaining on the road I was on. My departure became a source of hope. A few days later, we were called to sing in St. Peter's Square for a ceremony with Pope John Paul. I gazed out on the central plaza, onto the Via della Conciliazione and up at the porticos under the Vatican basilica, and asked myself whether I really wanted to trade all of this for California.

California. The word evoked the giant redwoods, the wild coast, the snow-covered Sierras. It was my land, my home. Would I leave all of these Roman historical marvels for my land, I asked myself. "Yes, in a minute," I said aloud. The person standing next to me glanced over to see whom I was talking to. I was determined. I was convinced. I knew what I had to do.

————

Father Jonathan was a priest from Los Angeles who was studying in Rome. His dynamic sermons about Catholic doctrine made him popular among the more conservative crowd in his parish. I had met him a few years before in California. He had been sent to Rome by his bishop and was staying near the Oblate house close to Via Casilina. I had sometimes seen him at school and we chatted periodically. I respected him since he seemed to be strong but kindly. I was seeking reassurances that I was doing the right thing in leaving. In the past I had talked with him about some of my difficulties with the Oblates and he had commiserated with me. I made an appointment to see him to discuss the latest developments.

I was announced: "Padre Giovanni, a visitor for you," and I went upstairs to his room. He was about forty-five years old, heavy-set, with black hair and thick black-rimmed glasses. We sat down and I proceeded to tell him the entire story.

"I think you are making the right decision," he said. "The Oblates have never shown you any care or concern. You have suffered too much. Go back to California and rest; I think there you'll find your path, not here. And I'll support you any way I can. You never got any support from them at all."

He went on in this vein for some time. Then he said, "What you need is affection," and rose to his feet. "Here, I'm going to give you a hug." He proceeded to embrace me, but did not let go as I expected he would. It was a long hug and I was confused. He was sweating; my cheek became wet from his. I didn't enjoy this embrace, and I didn't know what it meant or what he was going to do. I glanced at his bed and decided that if he moved me in that direction I would push him away. This had to be a misunderstanding. I had never seen him in that way.

A sudden announcement came over the intercom: "Padre Giovanni, your ride is downstairs."

"I wish we had more time," he said as he let me go. I thanked him for his time, and left. When I got back to St. Helen's, I took a shower to get rid of his sweat and his smell. Reflecting on the incident, it became clear to me that he had probably been sent to Rome because of sexual impropriety back in Los Angeles. I wondered why he had taken an apartment so close to the seminarians at St. Elena. It was an uncomfortable incident, but it was over and I would not revisit it.

The day before my departure, I whispered to Amadeo at his doorway, "I have something to show you, come to my room."

My room was now virtually empty, except for things that I didn't want to take. I was bringing only my essential possessions home. When Amadeo walked into my stark quarters, his eyes grew wide.

"I'm taking a year off and I wanted to let you know before I leave. Please don't tell anyone else."

He was silent for a moment, then he asked, "You're coming back, aren't you?"

"I don't know, I'm not sure."

"I know you're coming back," he said. "I'm not saying goodbye because I know you'll be back."

It was all set; the next day I would be in California just as I had dreamed.

Doors

—

I HAD A PLAN: I WOULD enroll in the university and not live with my parents. If I got into U.C. Berkeley I would move there; if not, I would go to the local university in Davis and stay with my grandmother. I knew that living with my parents would not work for me. The day after my arrival, I asked, "Dad, do you have that information about enrolling at Berkeley?"

His answer was no.

"Did you contact the university at all, like you said you would?" I asked, irritated.

"No, and where do you think you'll get the money for school anyway?"

I was already angry at him and it was only my second day at home. He hadn't contacted the university, and I should have known that since he hadn't supported me financially in Rome, he wouldn't begin to do it once I was here. How could I have expected or hoped for such an unlikely scenario? The registration for Berkeley should have been done the preceding November, and here it was June. There was no way I could be accepted. And after five years in the seminary, I was penniless.

I felt isolated in Modesto: my siblings were scattered, my old friends had moved on in their lives and attempts to renew those relationships proved formal and artificial. I was alone again. I had only myself to rely on and to communicate with. It would have to be enough.

I found a job as a busboy in a large ice cream parlor. The salary was minimal, but I could afford gasoline and some food. My co-workers were unsophisticated teenagers who had never left California. Their interests seemed petty and provincial to me, and a lot of the time I didn't even understand their language. I had traveled in Europe, experienced life-changing events, visited historical places and been exposed to foreign cultures. They were talking about their high-school math teacher, or the girls they had sex with when they were fifteen. It was suffocating, but I put on a false façade of contentment as I cleaned tables and washed dishes.

"It won't be long until you make waiter," the manager told me one day after I had been bussing tables for three months. I thought to myself that staying in this place was the last thing I wanted to do. This was not how I wanted to spend this year. This was not how I wanted to live. But what could I do? How could I move forward?

Some weeks later I told my father I was going to move in with my grandmother to help her out. That seemed acceptable to him; I had often stayed with her before. Even though she was sometimes difficult to get along with, for the most part she left me in peace. But I was intensely lonely. "I have no friends!" I cried in despair one day in my bedroom. It was true; I knew no one in Modesto I could call and spend time or talk with. I didn't know how to make new friends. At times I felt as if I would explode. I began to write poetry as a way to express my longing and depression. Perhaps depression is, in fact, a kind of longing. I wanted my life to get better, but I didn't know how to do it.

I told my father that I was going to quit working at the ice cream parlor and enroll at U.C. Davis as an extension student. "I can take classes there starting in late September. I earned enough money to pay for the first semester, so that's what I'm going to do."

He said that was fine. I was eager to quit my job and take a step forward; I hated the feeling of being stuck. Even though my future was uncertain, I hoped that one step would illuminate others to follow. For the moment I could live my dream of attending an American university.

I was happy to get back into the academic routine; academia was a world I felt comfortable in. The classes gave me structure and a sense of direction. I continued to feel depressed, however, unsure of what I wanted to do or should do with my life. I had no desire to try to involve myself in college activities, since this place was worlds away from what I was used to. It was simply somewhere to attend classes and then go home.

After several months the money I had earned was running out. I had to find another job. But what did I want to do? What would be fulfilling? What experience did I have that qualified me to do anything? I began to write to my friends back in Rome. Corresponding with them gave me a sense of belonging. I described things in California and they told me what was going on in the seminary. I found this comforting: life in the seminary was more familiar than my life at home, where I felt isolated from the culture around me because the Church had been my sole occupation.

Around Christmas I was offered a job as cook at a monastery of nuns in the wilderness, about an hour from Modesto. I wasn't sure whether I wanted to re-enter a church-related world so soon after the seminary, but I had no other options. Besides, there was a community college nearby, where I could continue to take classes. I told myself that perhaps this was the path I was somehow meant to follow. So I accepted and worked at the monastery for several months, cooking, cleaning and helping out in other ways. I wasn't unhappy there; though I still felt isolated, I suffered less intensely from loneliness. Even if it had no goal, here my life had a structure. Perhaps this would lead to something else; perhaps God would show me the next step.

After a few months, I received an unexpected offer to work at a parish in Modesto as an assistant. I would be back in a purely clerical world again, and I wasn't sure that this was the best thing for me. But I was convinced that nothing happened by chance and, once more, I had no other options, so I accepted the job and moved into the rectory. I had known the pastor, Msgr. O'Conner, since I was a child.

After a few days I settled in and the pastor said he wanted me to teach a Bible class for the parish. I told him that I didn't know enough about the Bible to do that and I had never taught adults before.

"You'll do fine; they don't know anything. Just teach what you learned in your classes in Rome."

I felt inadequate, but I used my class notes to develop a course in Biblical history and began the next week. The class consisted of about a dozen of the most pious women in the parish. They were certainly non-threatening, and after the first meeting, I found I enjoyed teaching and seemed to have a previously undiscovered talent for it.

As time went by, I entered into the pastor's daily routine, teaching and helping out at ceremonies. He was an Irish immigrant who had lived in his parish for over forty years. In fact, there were more Irish-born than American-born clergy in Modesto.

One day the pastor told me that I should just leave the Oblates and be a priest in Modesto. "You would be better off."

I was noncommittal. He kept pressuring me, but I couldn't decide. Summer was coming and I would have to make a decision. I had been away for almost a year now and even though I hadn't discovered the cause of my unhappiness, returning to the Oblates seemed the only logical thing to do. After a year away, things would be different and anyway I had found no other path to follow, no other viable way to live my life. It must have been God's will that I return to the seminary, since He had shown me no other path.

I phoned Father Manone. "This is Mark Tedesco from California," I began. "I'm calling to let you know that I'm ready to come back in August."

There was a pause. Then he said: "Mark, the superiors have decided rather negatively concerning your return."

"What! You mean not to return at all? Ever?"

He said yes, that was what he meant.

Overcome, in a cloud of confusion, darkness and panic, I quickly hung up. He had given no reason for the decision. I was dazed. How could I teach my class that night? I had been rejected by the seminary. I had no other path, no other life to live. What could I do? What should I do?

I kept the rejection to myself. I was ashamed; rejection must mean something was wrong with me. I wondered if I suffered from mental instability—perhaps that was why I was rejected. Who could I talk to about this? Who would understand my hurt and shame? I made a mental list of everyone I knew. The only one who could help me was the pastor. I tried to convince myself that the end of one thing could be the beginning of another, and went to Msgr. O'Conner. "Father, the Oblates told me not to return to their seminary. I'm really upset and depressed about it."

"Best thing that could ever happen to you!" he said cheerfully. But it didn't feel that way to me. I told him I didn't want to attend the local seminary for Modesto because there was a good deal of ideological contention there. He said he would talk with Father Schons about it. I had known Father Schons since high school where he had worked in the library. A few days later the pastor told me, "Father Schons is going to go to the bishop and ask that you be allowed to study for Modesto at the North American College seminary in Rome. If the bishop doesn't want to pay for it, we'll come up with the money." I was overjoyed. This might be the opening to a better path.

The bishop did indeed approve the suggestion and insisted that his office pay for my tuition. I would leave for Rome the following month to begin studies at the North American College, or NAC. A new adventure was about to begin. God was working for me again.

Caught in the storm

———

"WELCOME TO THE NORTH AMERICAN COLLEGE." The Rector addressed fifty of us in the seminary theatre in the college in September of 1984. "You are at the premier seminary of the United States; it is a privilege for you to be here and I hope you make the most of your time. Each one of you has been specifically chosen to come to the North American College. It will be a challenging time for you, but full of rewards. . . ." I knew I was not chosen to come here because I was the cream of the crop, but because Father Schons had arranged it for me. However it had happened, I was grateful to be back in Rome.

The Rector, Msgr. Purkelle, was from San Diego. He was about forty-five years old, with a great pile of graying brown hair. He went on, "We are here to follow our mission, our mission in life. We have this opportunity to do so here. The priesthood that we are called to is a way of following this mission, of serving others. . . ." He talked for another hour or so.

I said to the person next to me, Neil from Canada, "In this whole hour he has said nothing, no substance at all, just politically correct platitudes. What does he really think about anything?"

"He's a political animal," Neil said, "so he won't take a position on anything. You'll see."

The North American College, or NAC as it was called by the seminarians, was a residence and house of formation run by the American bishops; theology classes were held in various universities in Rome. We would live at the NAC, where we would attend conferences, receive counseling and be judged on whether we were worthy of ordination. It was a kind of proving ground and I would find that even before my arrival I had already been scrutinized, categorized, and judged.

Each of the new seminarians, or "new men" as they were called at the NAC, was assigned a priest on staff. We would eventually be able to choose our own mentors, but for now they were appointed. I was assigned to Father Donnel from Connecticut. He was in his late thirties, had red hair, and never wore socks. His nickname was "the Wounded Wounder," a play on the title of a popular spiritual book called *The Wounded Healer*. It was rumored that he was vicious to those whom he disliked, so I had my guard up at our first conference.

"I understand," he said, "that you did not leave the Oblates completely of your own choice. Are you here because you *have* to be here, or do you *want* to become part of this community, which is part of the larger American Church?"

"I'm here because I want to be here," I replied. I was already on the defensive, trying to convince him that I belonged.

I hadn't really been exposed to divisions in the Catholic Church; now I encountered them at the North American College. There were those who wanted an American Catholic Church that would be progressive, open-minded and reasonably independent from the Vatican; these were opposed by conservatives who considered themselves true Roman Catholics. These two camps detested each other. I soon realized that the priest staff at the NAC were on what could be called the American Catholic side, and they thought I was a conservative. This was not because of anything I said or did, but simply because I had been in the Oblates and the Oblates were reputed to be conservative.

The staff at the NAC had to walk a fine line; being in the shadow of the Vatican they had to appear to be more conservative than they actually were. We were forbidden to wear the cassock, the black robe, on the seminary grounds because this violated the spirit of the American Church, but when asked to do a service at the Vatican we were required to show up in the cassock. I came to see that it was all about appearances.

Many of the priests at the NAC who were charged with our formation saw their appointment there as a stepping-stone to a bishopric. These priests took advantage of their positions: they completed doctorates, got to know American bishops and cardinals, gave lectures and wrote articles. They were very careful to safeguard their reputations, and would not tolerate any seminarian speaking ill of them. I was surprised at this preoccupation with one's reputation and ecclesiastical career; I had never encountered it before. In this atmosphere of politics and intolerance at the North American College, I knew I would have to wend my way carefully. Very carefully.

———

It was early fall and the university had not yet opened. Since I knew Italian, I was excused from the Italian classes that were filling the days of the other "new men." I felt out of place. My history with the Oblates drew me to them. My Novitiate group had just been ordained priests. Several of them were going to have their first Mass at St. Elena and I decided to slip out and attend.

It was a strange sensation to walk into St. Elena. I knew every corner of this house that was no longer my home; I no longer had the right to go up the stairs to the chapel or the library. I felt disowned. I went into the church and the sacristy to see who was there whom I knew. I looked up to see Father Manone directly in front of me.

"*Ciao, Padre Manone,*" I greeted him. He froze, with a look of absolute shock and fear on his face. He was so uncomfortable that he was trembling and could not look at me.

"How are you? I'm at the North American College now," I said.

He seemed too distraught to answer and moved quickly away from me. I couldn't understand his behavior. Did his conscience bother him because he had dismissed me? I began to wonder if he had told Fr. Bergamo and the others that it was I who had decided not to return, instead of vice versa. Why else would he seem to be so terrified to see me? I left the sacristy perplexed and sat down for the Mass.

After the ceremony I stayed and chatted with my old companions with whom I felt at home. "You have to keep your mouth shut and go along with the system if you want to make it to ordination," Dave told me. Sitting on the bus to return to the NAC, I knew that he was right; I would have to try to fit in, not make waves, not criticize or object to anything. I would have to become just another face in the seminary crowd. This was my road.

In the Oblate seminary, the entire focus was on faith and on building one's spiritual life. If there was an exaggeration, it was on the side of those who had become so pious that they no longer seemed human. At the NAC, the topic of faith never came up; it was not considered an essential issue. If I was looking for some sort of reference point, some spiritual fountain to quench my thirst, it was clear that I would not find it here. Instead I found a divisive political atmosphere—precisely what I had wanted to avoid in choosing a seminary. As I got to know the other seminarians I was surprised at how relatively few seemed to be interested in spirituality. It was perplexing; were they here for an adventure? Did they want to become church leaders? Was it that they liked being looked up to in their communities? Why become a priest unless from a desire to share an experience of God? I couldn't understand it. I would have to find my own way, to seek a deeper path than the one that the NAC offered. It was like a desert and I needed water.

Another thing I noticed at the NAC was the large number of effeminate seminarians there. Some were openly homosexual. If there was any homosexuality in the Oblates, it was well hidden. Men there did not act like women. Once at lunch at the NAC one of the resident priests talked about oral sex; to demonstrate, he peeled a banana and moved it in and out of his mouth. Open sexuality, especially homosexuality, seemed shameful to me. How could anyone become comfortable with that, especially in this life we had chosen? I dared not talk about this to anybody; the subject made me extremely uncomfortable.

I was beginning to feel lost, without a reference point. Shortly before I left Modesto I had read a newspaper article about a movement in Italy called "Communion and Freedom." The movement was described in enthusiastic terms: thousands of young people were experiencing the Church as something alive and relevant, faith was intertwined with life, not divorced from it. The description intrigued me so much that I decided to seek out this movement and find out more about it. After several inquiries, I was given an appointment with Father Rodolfo, one of the CF leaders in Rome.

Father Rodolfo, or Don Rodolfo as he was called, was about forty years old, handsome, vibrant and intelligent. What impressed me about him was his complete removal from the divisiveness in the Catholic Church and his direct interest in me and my welfare. Even though I struggled to express it, he seemed to grasp immediately what I sensed was missing at the NAC and what I wanted in life.

"What do you think of this Father Luigino?" he asked. "Many Italians seem to be drawn to him. To me, he is not an appealing figure at all." Brother Luigino had become a priest while I was away in the United States.

"I don't know if he's for real or not," I replied. I really didn't care one way or the other about Luigino any longer. He had no more importance in my life than what I had eaten for dinner the night before. "What is this CF movement? I asked.

"Friendship. It's a road, a way of life."

"What's the next step?"

"Spend time with us. You can go to the meetings—which we call the community school—with the other seminarians. We'll continue to build a friendship together. And you can call or come to see me any time."

I left that meeting feeling that he understood me more than I understood myself up to that point. I felt a joyful sense of promise that I had not felt in years.

A few days later the entire seminary was taken out of town on a retreat. I became almost obsessed with this meeting with Don Rodolfo. What would it mean? What would it bring? Is it the path I have been looking for? Did I find someone who was actually interested in my welfare? I couldn't wait to get back to Rome to find out. I was hopeful I could discover that adventuresome road I had longed for since I was in high school.

The community school Don Rodolfo mentioned was at the Roman College near the Pantheon. The other seminarians at that college were all Italians, mostly from the north, and they immediately embraced me as their friend. Since I had no idea what this CF was, they asked me to come to their weekly meetings when they would read and reflect on a text chosen by this Movement, which was headquartered in Milan. Its leader was a Father Guardini whom I had never heard of. They were studying his writings. I had some trouble understanding Guardini's Italian. "Don't worry," Michele, one of the Italians, said. "It's hard for us to understand too." I could see they had a friendly sense of belonging. I wanted to discover more about this movement and what it could mean for me. I decided I would come every week.

A few days later there was a knocking at my door, and I was told that the Rector would like to see me. I felt intimated by Msgr. Purkelle. He had the authority to send me home tomorrow; to refuse me ordination. He had control over my life.

"Mark," he said, "I want to welcome you to the North American College. Your experience here will be much different than at the Oblates and I want to make sure you can leave that behind and embrace our life. Your seminary was probably more rigid; here you are freer and so have more responsibility. The spirituality is also different. But this is what the American bishops want. We are forming priests according to their directives and not according to the Oblates."

"You make it sound as if my time in the Oblates was a liability. I think of it more as an asset, something that I can use for my future."

"Yes, yes, but this is your community here. The American Church is where you'll be serving. I want to make an observation. You give the impression of being too clerical. I have noticed your clothes are drab. You need to wear more colors."

I didn't know if he was joking. I had never paid much attention to my clothes and had never thought about color one way or the other. He somehow read into my clothing choices a conservatism that was unwelcome here.

On my way back to my room, I met Jim from Canada who was often lurking around to get the latest scoop on whatever was happening. I told him he would never guess what the Rector had just told me. To my surprise Jim took this very seriously.

"I think you shouldn't take this lightly," he said. "Your staying here might be on the line. You have to make them think you're not the type of person they imagine you to be. Come downstairs with me."

We went to a room filled with discarded clothes from former students. Jim handed me a very colorful sweater, saying, "Here, wear this whenever you can." He found other shirts and sweaters and helped me carry a great pile of them to my room. Jim was from Toronto and he was in my class. He was someone I felt comfortable with, someone who was on my side. "You need to work on your image," he continued. "Join our music group; we do lots of folk music and that will really throw them off."

Even though my singing ability was minimal, I did join the group. I also decided to grow a beard, as another way to break out of the mold of that conservative Catholic group that they had cast me in. I dressed as colorfully as I could, wearing the bright sweaters Jim had found for me. I also began singing with the folk group, even though I had to struggle to carry a tune. After some weeks went by, I felt more confident that I could play this game, if that was what it would take.

When I had been at the NAC for a month, I received a message on the corridor phone: there was a visitor at the main gate for me. I wasn't expecting any guests, but when I went to the gate, I found Marcus waiting for me. We hadn't been in touch because he was still at home when I left for Rome. We went up to my room together. "You won't believe what I've been through!" he told me.

He had gone home that summer to be with his family. "I told the bishop that I wanted to study for the Modesto diocese and complete my education in Rome. He said that he wouldn't send me to Rome, but that I could join the diocese and go to the local seminary. I told him I would never go there. He said it wouldn't be possible for me to go to Rome for the Modesto diocese. All he had to do was say yes! What would it have cost him?

I asked him about *you*, why *you* got to come here. He said he didn't know how you slipped through. But he said he wouldn't send me to Rome under any circumstances. So I came back on my own. I'm not an Oblate, I just came back on my own and my parents are going to support me while I'm here."

I was stunned at his situation, but not surprised. Marcus had never really been happy in the Oblates, preferring to be in Modesto with his family. I think he had wanted to leave the Order some years before, but felt trapped because he had made vows and believed that if he left he would be going against God's will. That's how Marcus was. He always tried to follow all the rules. As he talked on about his situation, I started to wonder if the bishop of Modesto had really been wrong to refuse to send Marcus back to Rome. Marcus's family had always granted his every wish, and he seemed to expect that response from everyone. I couldn't help thinking that this might be God's way of breaking down Marcus's need to be in control all the time. Real change often occurs when one is forced to deal with situations one can't control. I thought that this challenge might actually be Marcus's chance really to follow God's will if he would accept the bishop's decision.

"So," he continued, "can I stay with you for a few days until I can find a place to live?"

He had come here without any prior notice or discussion. My position at NAC was already extremely precarious. It had obviously not occurred to him that his staying here could place me at risk. But I couldn't turn him away. I went down to Jim's room for consultation. "Put him in one of the empty rooms on the third floor," Jim said. "Tell him to leave in the morning before seven and come back late at night. If anyone questions him, tell him to say that he's my guest, not yours." It was good advice, and I took it.

A few weeks later Marcus was able to find a place to stay. But I was upset. Had Marcus raised a doubt about me in my bishop's mind when he used my example to facilitate his own return to Rome? The bishop had sent me here, yes, but his response to Marcus seemed to imply that he might consider that to have been an oversight, which meant that he could call me back at any moment. My life in Rome was completely dependent on the bishop's whim, so I couldn't be sure how long I would be here. I had a terrible feeling of insecurity about the present as well as the future. I tried to deal with this by imagining that I placed a particular worry or issue into a box that I closed, sealed and pushed into the corner of an attic.

There! I thought to myself, I won't be bothered by that for a while.

———

At the NAC, there were groups of students who associated with one another on the basis of geography—being from the same diocese. Or of ideology—having the same theological inclination. Since coming from the Oblates labeled me as a conservative, I soon found myself in the midst of people with that tendency. I was continually being warned: "Be careful what you say to the Rector! Be *very* careful of Father Donnel; he's a snake! Don't ever mention the word Pope or Vatican! Don't let anyone see you praying the rosary here!" I was admonished repeatedly on how to play this game.

"Some guys are closet conservatives, like Dave," Neil told me one day. Apparently some seminarians with traditional preferences were able to fit in by keeping their inner life secret. I seemed to be in the middle of a microcosm of a sick and divided church.

The name of Father Donnel continually came up as one to be reckoned with and he did, in fact, strike me as cold, calculating and narrowly ideological. We had to choose a permanent mentor or advisor at the NAC to meet with every month. He was to be our reference point in the clerical community; any conversation with him was confidential, so he couldn't participate in discussions or voting on the person under his charge. Donnel had been my temporary advisor. The conservatives continually counseled me to choose him as my permanent mentor so that I could silence him. Otherwise, they said, he would surely be against me when the time came to vote for ordination. I took that advice. Donnel seemed flattered that I had chosen him. If he only knew why, I thought. I knew the meetings with him would be unpleasant, but it was one price to pay to increase my chances of making it through.

Being a student at the North American College was to become a member of a Catholic subculture of aspiring church leaders. I had noted this in the faculty shortly after my arrival, but now I saw the same attitude in many of the students. There was a preoccupation with building up one's ecclesiastical

resume and reputation and an effort to control others' percep-
tions of oneself even among the seminarians. This created a
stifling atmosphere.

The college also tended to be a studiedly American enclave.
On site was a store stocking all American products; there was
also a money-exchange bureau, computer center and library.
It wasn't really necessary to go out the front gate to Rome
at all. There was a note-taking system in place at the Gregorian University, so many of the men didn't even attend classes.
In fact, most of the seminarians learned little or no Italian in
their three or four years at the college. I was repelled by these
aspirations to church leadership and by living in an American
colony. Once Jim came to my room, agitated and concerned.
"Mark," he said, "you should be more careful to fit into the
American community here. Become a more visible part. Stay in
more; you're always going out into the city to meet your Italian
friends. You need to integrate more into NAC."

I laughed. "Jim, my life *starts* at that front gate, and on the
other side of it!"

Perhaps I would never fit in completely. I wasn't willing to
give up Rome to do that.

The year proceeded, classes began, and the Oblate experience faded from my horizon. I began to enjoy my relative
freedom both to explore the city and to participate in the Communion and Freedom movement. I learned to balance between
being politically correct at the North American College and
following the CF path. Father Rodolfo became my reference point and the Italian seminarians at the Roman College
became my community. I had begun to find a way to live and
grow in my new situation.

Before Fr. Rodolfo, I had never met a priest whom I had
truly admired and respected. He seemed to combine all the
qualities I had sought and never found in religious men I had
met in the past; he was human but deeply spiritual. He never
wasted words, always went directly to the heart of the matter

in two or three sentences. He became a model for me. This gave me strength and hope, since I had felt disillusioned with several of the Oblate priests and didn't trust those at the NAC. Rodolfo showed me that to be a priest, one must first be a man. I hoped to grow to be like him.

As the months passed, I felt more relaxed about my stay in Rome. Now that I had come this far it would be unreasonable for my bishop to call me back and interrupt my studies here. I didn't like NAC, but I was in Rome. The city began to take on a more human quality for me. Instead of seeing magic everywhere, I started to feel as if I were a part of its great history, its stones and monuments, its people and its art. This was beautiful. I was feeling more content now, more at peace. Soon summer came, classes ended and I looked forward to starting the next academic year.

YEAR 8

Coming to Life

———

ON MY RETURN TO ROME IN 1985, I resolved to immerse myself more deeply in the Communion and Freedom movement. It offered me a path. The essence of the movement seemed to be that human nature longs for a fulfillment that only an infinite presence can fill. This presence in history has a name: Christ, and can be encountered within the community that recognizes Him. Faith is not divorced from life, but rather everything is caught up within its mystery. Faith is no longer relegated to the sphere of spirituality but incarnates all of life. Though this was the theological viewpoint, what most attracted me was the normality of those in the movement. Father Rodolfo was just one example; all the CF members seemed wholeheartedly faithful to the Church and yet had any number of human interests and concerns. In the Oblates, it seemed that the more pious a person became, the more he was removed from any other interests. The path of CF seemed more true to me, more appealing, more beautiful and fulfilling.

In my previous religious experience, "human" was equated with the "flesh" and the "Divine" with the "spirit." Since the spirit must overcome the flesh, the human had to be subdued by the Divine. The division between the human world and God's world was absolute, so to approach God man must abandon his humanity. That is what I had thought and it was the way I had attempted to live. The CF held that the Divine and the

125

human are as compatible as an answer is to a question. Nothing in oneself had to be abandoned or rejected since humanity is both a road to, and a reflection of, the Divine. Spirituality would become alienation unless it was lived as a response to what one really desired as a man or a woman. As I came to accept this, my friendship grew with Father Rodolfo and the community at the Roman College.

On Sunday mornings there was a Mass for CF at Santa Maria in Trastevere. I found it fascinating to see the ancient church overflowing with people. These were not old pious women, as in most Roman churches, but young university students among others, forming a lively and friendly community. I found the sermons moving: they were not filled with pious platitudes but with real human experience. The music was mysterious and beautiful, some ancient and some contemporary. I was drawn there every week to be part of that enchanting experience with my other friends from CF.

As I found myself more and more engrossed, I wanted to share my feelings with others at the North American College. I didn't keep my participation in the movement secret from Father Donnel or the seminary community. I thought that inviting others to the Mass in Trastevere could be a way to unite my connection to the movement with the NAC. I wouldn't feel so divided if some others in the seminary participated in the movement with me. So I put a notice on the bulletin board next to all the elevators at the college: "Come and experience the CF movement; meet at 11 a.m. to attend the Mass of the movement in Trastevere." I was excited; perhaps ten or twenty people would attend. I was sure they would be as blown away as I was by what they saw.

Sunday arrived and I eagerly prepared to lead the group from the NAC to the Mass. After all, Rome was filled with interesting faith communities and experiences that could never be found back in the United States. It was as if the Church here still retained, in some places, an element of the spirit of its earliest centuries that had given strength to martyrs joyfully to give over their lives.

I went down to the front gate twenty minutes early to make sure I wouldn't miss anyone coming down. By eleven o' clock no one had showed up. Thinking that they might have misunderstood the meeting place, I circled the grounds to the back gate. It was now 11:15, and I was going to be late. I dashed out down the street towards the church. Not one person had come. It was as if no one was interested in faith, I thought. But then, why should they be? The NAC was not about faith, it was about politics. I decided that from now on, I would focus exclusively on CF as the community I wanted to belong to. The NAC would only be the place where I lived. Nothing more.

One day Marcus came to visit me again. He had found a place to live on the metro line outside Rome as an independent student. "I'm thinking that maybe I will go back to the Oblates at the end of this year," he began.

"No," I protested, "don't do that just because you have no alternative!"

"We'll see. What else can I do? The bishop only had to say yes, so now Modesto is impossible. But anyway, I didn't come to talk to you about that. You got out of the Oblates just in time, Mark. Father Luigino is a fake. They have witnesses, seminarians and nuns, who say they were molested by him. Perfumes were found in his room that he used to make that scent. The Italians still believe in him and the Americans don't, so the Oblate order is completely divided. And San Vittorino has been shut down!" he said, emphatically.

I was surprised. Luigino really meant nothing to me anymore, but I asked where he was.

"Right now he's in Vienna while the investigation is continuing. They say he's going to leave the Oblates and found his own Order—something like the 'Slaves of the Immaculate Heart of Mary' and all the Italians are going to join him."

It really did seem that I had gotten out just in time. I asked Marcus why he wanted to go back under these circumstances.

"It's better than being on my own. And maybe it's God's will; after all, I made vows with the Oblates."

I didn't agree with him, but we were no longer close; he was leading his own life. I still thought he would be better off back in California doing what the bishop had asked him to do. I thought that God was working in his life, giving him an opportunity, pulling him beyond himself. But he said, "The only way for me to stay in Rome is to return to the Oblates; going back to California to study is out of the question. . . ."

I didn't quite know how to reconcile everything I had experienced at San Vittorino with this new information that Luigino was a charlatan. I suddenly saw in a new light those times alone with him when he embraced me and pulled up my shirt. In any event, I didn't need miraculous signs any more. I was looking for a more human experience of faith now; focusing solely on the Divine had mired me in depression.

———

It is easy to imagine that one's life has changed when the externals have changed. The North American College was a different world from what I had been accustomed to, but soon the depression lifted that had enveloped me in the Oblates, although I still wanted affection and validation. The students at the NAC were colder, more distant and calculating, than the Latins. I became friendly with some of the Italian workers at the college: Giuseppe the doorman, Guiglio in the laundry and Renaldo in the kitchen. There was an emotional resonance that I experienced with the Italians that I didn't find with the Americans. But although I felt drawn to the Italians, I didn't form the kind of exclusive and close friendship with any of them that I had had with Amadeo. I had resolved not to focus exclusively on another again; I was unwilling to lose my sense of balance.

Some of the American seminarians noticed my friendship with the Italian workers and ridiculed me for it. It didn't matter to me. People were people, and just because one is studying to be a priest and the other washes clothes didn't make either person any more or less worthy. Some days I would linger at the front gate for long conversations about life with Giuseppe, and Giuglio would have me over for dinner and invite me to stay with his family in Sardinia. I was beginning to have a feeling of belonging, even at the North American College.

As I continued to participate in the CF Movement, it seemed to me that in this experience I might find an answer to both my intellectual and emotional longings. Perhaps the war within might give way to peace. Maybe there was something in this movement that could answer that craving of my whole being. Thus, the movement became a path that I walked with enthusiasm and gratitude. The more I participated, the more it seemed to be a life-long road. It might be the cord that would bind my existence together.

Father Rodolfo was a busy man, but when I felt confused or discouraged I could call him and he always made time to see me. For him Christianity was an adventure; it was not a set of laws or beliefs but a new life and a new perspective. I was also struck by the fact that he seemed so non-judgmental of other people's choices.

I was invited to lunch at the seminary where he lived with other CF members. One of the lunch guests was a famous Italian pop singer whom Rodolfo had known for years. They shared a friendship even though their attitudes toward life were completely different. During the conversation the singer said, "I've finally separated sex from love and realized that the one can have nothing to do with the other." Rodolfo did not moralize about this, but commented with a smile, "I'm sorry for your wife." It struck me that Rodolfo's comment had sprung from his humanity, his concern for the feelings of another, not from a moral judgment based on certain rules. I wanted to develop this openness of spirit, without prejudices.

Ninety-eighty-five, my second year at the North American College, continued to be filled with political intrigue which would soon reach a head. I had completed my bachelors degree the previous year and I was to begin a two-year program, equivalent to the American masters degree, at the John Paul II Institute for Marriage and Family. I had chosen this school because it was new, only in its second year of operation, and the professors, some of whom were members of CF, seemed enthusiastic, animated and involved. Finally, there were laymen teaching there, with wives and families; at the other pontifical institutes, all the professors were priests. This place was new, exciting and I wanted to be part of it.

I had not expected to provoke a crisis when I told the Rector and other faculty where I wanted to attend graduate school. I quickly learned that the problem was not that the school was called the Institute for Marriage and Family, but that it was named for John Paul II. Since the school had been directly founded by the Pope and was administered by the Vatican, it was seen as backward and conservative.

The Rector and seminary staff could not object to someone going to a pontifical institute without consequences to their own ecclesiastical careers. They had to find a way to stop me from going without directly criticizing the Institute itself. They stopped my application process and called an emergency meeting to talk about the situation. I was asked to hold back on my graduate school plans. I waited. My life was once more totally in the hands of others.

The crisis lasted three days, during which my continued presence at the NAC was called into question. Jim was supportive, spending a good deal of time with me in my room while we waited to see what my fate would be. My bishop was telephoned, a representative from the North American College was sent to the Institute to investigate it, and my private records were examined.

Early on the third day, the Rector told me to stand by; he was going to give me a response. I stayed in my room all day, waiting to be called, fearing that I had made a grave mistake in choosing the John Paul II Institute, and that I might be sent back to the United States because of it. Finally, after this agonizing wait, I was called to the Rector's quarters around eight that night.

The Rector lived on the floor below mine in a four-room suite with beautiful hardwood floors, tapestries, comfortable furniture upholstered in red, and a sweeping view of Rome. He sat in a red-and-gold chair; I seated myself on a sofa.

"Mark," he began, gazing at the ceiling, "we value your desire to attend the John Paul II Institute; that's what I want to say first of all. The faculty here have met and spoken about what is best for you, for Mark. You are the focus of our concern. You haven't been back in your diocese very often since you were with the Oblates. And you know a lot of Italians in the city because you lived here for so long. We think, therefore, that it would be best for you that you attend, not the John Paul II Institute, but the Alphonsianum. There are others from your year attending the Alphonsianum and going to the same university with them would help you to integrate yourself more into our community.

"We also believe that this whole incident demonstrates that you have a problem with obedience, so we would ask you to go to the Psychological Center at the Gregorian University twice a week for counseling this year. That is the decision that we have made."

I knew that if I did not accept this, my stay in Rome would be terminated immediately. "Thank you," I said. "I do want to be part of this community, and I do have friends here at the NAC, who have, by the way, been in my room all day supporting me as I waited for your call. As for my diocese of Modesto, I do know it well, since I was born and raised there. And I do accept your recommendation."

After leaving his suite I immediately called Father Rodolfo to tell him about this three-day crisis. "Why didn't you call me sooner?" he asked. "You don't have to deal with all this alone."

I was stunned. I hadn't called him sooner because I really didn't think he had time to care about what I was enduring at NAC. But he did. That surprised me. "Come and see me when you're able and we can talk about it," he continued. I hung up feeling better. I had some support. I was not alone.

A week later classes started at the Alphonsianum. It was an institute of moral theology under the Lateran University, housed in an old black smog-mantled building with one large classroom or *aula* on the main floor and several smaller classrooms upstairs. The university was run by the Redemptorist order of priests; so all the professors were clergy. I attended the lecture classes for two weeks, during which all the instructors simply read from their notes, verbatim. Since the notes could be purchased in the bookstore, I stopped taking my own notes and simply underlined passages as the professors spoke.

After several weeks of this, I couldn't see any point in attending class every day, so I began to skip a day or two. After about a month I attended class only once every two weeks. I found the lectures so boring and dated that I couldn't even make myself stay for the entire class period. I simply stayed long enough to see where we were in the notes, and when the professor looked down to read, I slipped out. I went to class three or four times a week at the end of the semester, and made sure to ask a question or two, so the professor would recognize my face at the final exam. I felt that the whole thing was simply a waste of time.

I sat in on some classes at the John Paul II Institute and found them absorbing. There was something new here: a deeper point of view, a new experience of theology and anthropology which made the lessons exciting. One professor was a member of the European Parliament, another, a husband and father, came from Lublin University in Poland; another was a priest from the CF Movement in Milan. The classes were

interesting: anthropological discussions on interpersonal communion; Christian and non-Christian traditions of marriage
and family; evolution of theology from natural law to person-
alism, etc. They were all theoretical topics with practical appli-
cations, investigating the way we look at ourselves and others.

At the Alphonsianum, the students were all priests or
seminarians; at the Institute they came from all walks of life:
married, single, priests, nuns, college kids. It seemed to me
unfortunate that the NAC should be closed to this interesting
and innovative experience. But I had to survive there so I knew
I must choose my battles wisely.

Everyone at the Alphonsianum complained about how
boring and abstract the lectures were. When the second term
began I decided not to choose my classes by their content, since
I found none of them stimulating, but rather according to their
scheduled time. In this way I was able to arrange *all* of my
classes for just two days a week, and since attendance was neither enforced nor necessary, I could simply pop into the classrooms a few times a month.

The exams at the Alphonse (as it was called) were all oral,
and after taking oral exams in Rome for years I had learned the
system. One class was called "Worldly Goods in the Writings
of John the Evangelist." Since I found this course irrelevant,
I hadn't really followed it, but I had to get a passing grade. I
found a three-page article that the professor had written on a
similar theme, and read it the morning of the exam.

When I came into the room, I told him how much I had
enjoyed his article. His face lit up. But, I said, there were a few
points that I wasn't sure I understood. I proceeded to quiz *him*
about the article and he enthusiastically answered my questions at length. Before we knew it the fifteen-minute testing
time had passed.

"I can see that you know the material well," he said, glancing at his watch. I shook his hand and thanked him for an
interesting course and discussion.

I got an A-plus in that course even though I really didn't know anything about it. I didn't feel guilty about this. At the Marriage Institute I was learning more in one session than I could learn in a whole term at the Alphonsianum, and I was put off too by the fact that the Alphonse was infected by that disease that contaminated most pontifical universities: indifference.

Many of the professors in Rome during the Second Vatican Council were brilliant experts in their specific fields, contributed greatly to the Council documents and published important theological works. But they did not relate to their students. Their notes were published in Latin, their hour lectures were read, no examples were given, and questions were not permitted. It was as if, for them also, attending classes was a necessary evil. Was teaching their penance for past sins?

I had a problem too with the topics of each class, which never related to any others. A professor might be the world authority on the theology of the Liturgy in Milan in 1555 and yet have no idea of what was being taught in the next room on moral theology during the same period. They didn't seem to have a grasp of the total picture of knowledge. Attending the Alphonse was a penance for me too.

I juggled my time among the Alphonsianum, the Marriage Institute, the Psychological Center at the Gregorian University, and my Latin homework. I had to work in two visits a week to the psychologist, so I chose two afternoons when I was usually too tired to do anything productive. At the Centro, as the Psychological Center was called, the method was nondirectional: the client was, in essence, his own counselor. Each session lasted one hour and the therapist—a student, not yet a certified therapist—did not counsel or even comment; he just listened and took notes. If I had nothing to say, he simply sat and stared at me.

This created pressure to have something to talk about, or else endure a long, awkward silence. I resented being forced to go to the Centro, especially on the pretext that I had a problem with obedience because I wanted to go to the Institute. But I decided to try to make the best of it and hope that something positive could come out of it.

My therapist was a dark-haired Australian who wore heavy black-rimmed glasses. I wasn't really able to get to know him. At times I engaged in small talk, wondering if he found it as dull as I did. Once I thought I saw him suppress a yawn. As time went on, I began to take the experience more seriously and to bring up some events from the past and even the present. I discussed my experience in the Oblates and at the North American College. I began to reveal some of my feelings, but not my inner core or self; having been forced into therapy, I didn't completely trust him. At times I talked about my emotional needs, but I wasn't able to resolve anything. Since I got so little response from the counselor, the method of the Centro became clear: heal thyself. The more one communicated one's inner life, the more one would be able to understand and integrate it. At least, that was the theory.

———

As I started to enjoy the city, my longing for the Oblate community dissipated. Even though the NAC had its drawbacks, all of Rome was before me with relatively few restrictions. One day I was offered a paid position at Vatican Radio as a translator, a job that required some late-night work. I immediately accepted, feeling the offer to be a privilege. The work itself in the main involved more English than Italian. I listened to live broadcasts of the Pope visiting English-speaking communities in Africa, and noted any changes he made to the written speeches I had before me. Some nights I worked as late as three in the morning; walking home in the streets of Rome at that hour, I didn't feel edgy as I would in a big American city: crime in Rome was petty, not violent. I had never felt unsafe in Rome, never feared a mugging or a shooting. As I walked up the hill to the college I took a short cut and saw three or four cars, windows filled with steam. The Italians inside were having sex.

I saw more open sexuality in Rome than I had ever seen in the United States. One evening in a TV commercial for bathroom tile, I saw a woman come out in a robe, drop it to the floor, and take a shower in a full frontal nudity shot. Romans frequently had sex in public places: parks, busses, cars, beaches.

My first experience of this was in fact on a bus riding back to the college from the Vatican. Roman busses tend to be very crowded and I learned to watch my wallet and to hold on tight if I couldn't get a seat. On this day I was holding on, trying to keep my balance as the bus swerved sharply. We were all pushed back and the man standing in front of me was shoved against me. But when everybody moved away, his body remained against mine. Feeling confusion, panic and a certain enjoyment, I missed my stop. Was it because I was distracted, enjoying the experience? No, I told myself, I can't feel this way. I can't take pleasure in forbidden territory. I assured myself that it would never happen again. But I wondered what would have happened if I had stayed on the bus . . .

My emotional need began to manifest itself as sexual desire, but I was determined not to act on it, at least intentionally. One day when it was especially strong, I took that bus hoping that the experience would repeat itself. Needless to say, it did not. I was especially relieved that it did not when I heard a voice from the back of the bus: "Mark, what are you doing here?" I turned to see a group of nuns I knew, smiling and waving at me. "I'm going home," I replied, and that is what I did.

Pursuing sexual experiences can be sexuality plain and simple, but my emotional need fed into my sexual drive. I had an almost desperate need for love and affection, whether physical or emotional or both. I didn't know how to fill these needs because I didn't want to become sexually active. But I was desperate for love and in search of that peace which can come from finding and uniting with a loved one.

"You gotta see this," Jim said, laughing, as he entered my room. The NAC was a U-shaped building, so it was possible to see into the windows of the block of rooms on the other side. The far wing housed American priests who had come to Rome to take a short course in theology—in reality it was an extended vacation. "Come here and look." Jim pointed to a window across and down one floor from mine. Though the shades were partially drawn, it was possible to see the figure of a man masturbating on his bed. Jim thought it was funny. I was shocked but I found the sight fascinating.

Thomas, another seminarian from my class, knocked and came in and the three of us spent a few moments watching. Suddenly the person on the bed got up and walked toward his door. Because of the angle we could see only his legs. Moments later another set of legs walked to his window and pulled the shades all the way down. We looked at each other. "I wonder what's happening in that room right now," Jim said, "He does it every night, I've seen him."

I was surprised. I had never been exposed to any sexual activity in the seminary before, either in the Oblates or the NAC. It might have happened all the time or this might have been unusual, I didn't know. I found the whole incident curious.

————

Months went by and life settled into a routine: participating in the house schedule, studying in the mornings, attending the challenging classes in Latin letters in the afternoons and studying again in the evenings. Latin was so demanding that it took most of my study time and I wasn't always able to keep up with my theology classes. Besides studies, I felt a spiritual need. In the Oblates I had had a habit of setting aside one hour each day for silent prayer. Now with the seminary schedule and the study load, I didn't have enough time in the day to fit it all in.

After the first of the year I began to set my alarm at 4:30 in the morning, to shower and go to the chapel for my prayer hour, followed by the community Mass at six. This gave me the extra time I needed to complete all my daily tasks. In the afternoons I felt tired. Another student suggested I set my alarm and take a five-minute nap so that I could study refreshed. I tried that, but when I woke after five minutes I was even more tired than before. I tried to go to bed earlier, but it was difficult in such a busy place. I continued to get up early to get a jump on the day.

After some weeks on my new schedule, I came down with a cold. I had had many colds before and always kept a good stock of cold remedies in my room. I took some of these, but they didn't help. After a week in which I didn't seem to be getting better, Jim insisted that I see a doctor. But I thought that it was only a cold, all I needed was rest. I felt absolutely terrible, had no appetite at all and barely slept. I was hot too, but I didn't have a thermometer. Finally Jim said, "I'm bringing the *infirmarian* here after lunch whether you like it or not." The *infirmarian* was a seminarian who had studied some medicine and was in charge of dispensing medications.

"Come in," I groaned as the door opened on a group of seminarians. The *infirmarian* walked in and took one look at me. "We need to get him up to the infirmary *now*. We're getting a doctor here to see you today," he said to me firmly. I felt relieved; I had no idea what was happening to me, and I was surprised to find how weak I had become. I needed help to walk to the elevator.

In Italy there are public hospitals and private clinics. The public hospitals are notorious, but they're free. The clinics charge fees for service. The NAC had an arrangement with a private clinic with a British staff. Later that afternoon I was examined by Dr. Margaret, a gray-haired, kindly woman with a fascinating accent. She told me, "It could be several things; for the moment I suspect hepatitis. Let me start you on an antibiotic and I'll come see you in a few days. In the meantime you must eat and drink." This uncertain diagnosis worried me. "Mark, you must eat," the nun insisted as she pushed food at me at dinner. I tried but couldn't swallow more than a few pieces of orange.

The next morning I felt a bit better. "Maybe all you needed was the antibiotic," Jim said hopefully. I told him I needed to get better; I didn't want to fall behind in my studies.

But that night I seemed to have a relapse, and the next morning I felt even worse. The *infirmarian* told me, "The doctor says you must come to the hospital at once. There's a car waiting for you below; we'll help you." Now it took two men to help me to the car. Within minutes I was at the clinic; half an hour later I was in the X-ray room.

"You have pneumonia," the *dottoressa* said when I was back in my hospital bed. "We will start you on intravenous antibiotics immediately. You should start to feel better within a day or two." I was relieved to get a definite diagnosis.

The *dottoressa* told me that I was on complete bed rest, and couldn't get up even to go to the bathroom. Apparently, in Italian hospitals, the patient had to stay in bed as long as possible. Any movement could cause a relapse. Drafts especially were to be avoided at all costs. Of course without exercise it was difficult for me to regain my strength.

In the days that followed I had visitors: many of my friends from the CF community at the Roman College, and some from the North American College. My Latin professor showed up and told me not to worry about the class. Jim came and made me laugh so much so that one day I accidentally pulled out my IV. Shortly before I left the hospital the Rector of the NAC come to visit; somehow he always put me on my guard, as if I were being evaluated even then.

The days were getting warmer, Easter was approaching and I was feeling better and restless. On the ninth day I told the *dottoressa* that I wanted to finish recuperating at home. "I would like to keep you here another three or four days," she said. "But since it is almost Easter, I can discharge you only if you promise me you will stay in bed for one more week."

Of course I promised. So on day ten, I went back to the NAC. I did intend to stay in bed, but it was so sunny and green and bright. Spring was in the air. I felt as if I was just coming back to life. A walk over to the Vatican can't hurt, I said to myself. Since it was now Holy Week, St. Peter's would be bustling with activity and I wanted be part of that. In the basilica, pilgrims were everywhere: sightseeing, attending Mass, standing in line to go to confession. It was good to be back in this place, breathing this air, absorbing this atmosphere. I was happy, I was free, I was here.

Standing by one of the side altars, absorbed in my warm thoughts, I was suddenly horrified to see the *dottoressa*, whom I had solemnly promised I would stay in bed, standing in front of me in line waiting to go into the crypt. My heart jumped. Apparently she had not seen me. I slipped out and hobbled home, relishing my escape, enjoying the Holy Week sunshine of Rome.

Over the next month my strength slowly returned. I was anxious to resume my studies, but there was a lesson in this long sickness that would not be lost on me. I had a strong will and my spirit could dominate my flesh, mind over matter. But was this the way that I wanted to live? Was this a way I *could* live? My body failed me because I didn't consider it to be a real part of who I was. This had proved to be a mistake. I would have to live so that my flesh was not divorced from my spirit; neither one suppressing the other. I would need to find a way to be whole. It was the same dichotomy I had been wondering about for several years: can the Divine and the human be one? Can the flesh and spirit be united, or would they always be at war? I could not live as a divided person.

———

A few weeks into my recovery I sat down at the table for lunch and got into a discussion with some American seminarians about the Italian culture in which we were living. The longer I stayed in Rome the more I had come to appreciate the Italian relish for life as opposed to the American mere acceptance of it. I couldn't put this difference into words until one day John, a year ahead of me, told about an incident earlier in the week.

"There's a clothing store near the Vatican on Borgo Pio where a lot of guys go to get their pants. They have a great selection with good quality and prices. I started chatting with the owner about his business. I asked him, 'Why don't you sell shirts and shoes and not just pants?' Do you know what he said? 'If I did that, there would *always* be somebody in here.' Can you believe that? He actually doesn't want more business than he has!" John was incredulous. The owner was content to make a living without a lot of stress. As long as he made enough for his family's needs he was content and had no desire to expand his business to make more money.

A few weeks later I told Pino, from the Roman College, about the incident. He told me a similar story about a man sleeping in a hammock under a tree on a beautiful Lugurian beach where the deep-blue water lapped against the white sand. It was a warm summer day. Next to his hammock, holding a cold drink, was a hand-carved table, with inlaid wood. A tourist walking by stopped and asked the man if he had made the table. When the man said he had, the tourist commented on its quality and suggested the man make another one and sell it. "Then," the tourist said, becoming enthusiastic, "you could use the money to make three or four more and sell them and then you could make twenty or thirty tables, with chairs to match."

The man in the hammock looked perplexed. The tourist, becoming more animated, went on to tell him that if he sold those twenty or thirty, he could open a factory and sell them all over Italy and be head of the company. The man in the hammock shrugged. But the tourist had worked himself into a state of excitement. "Don't you see," he almost shouted, "then you could start an international corporation and sell tables, chairs, furniture, in America and all over the world! You would be rich!"

"And then what would I do?"

"Well, you could just sit back and enjoy yourself all day."

The man looked at him, and said, "*Ecco*, I am already enjoying myself all day." He put his hat over his eyes, and went back to sleep.

"That is the difference in mentality you are talking about," Pino said.

———

A few months after my hospital release I would be returning to America and I looked forward to going home, mostly to build up my strength. The coming fall would herald my final year in Rome; I would be finished with my degree and would be voted for (or against) ordination. I decided to take out a loan in California so that I could make the most of my final year: travel, dine out, do all those things I had wanted to do but never had the money to do.

Pandora Returns

———

My summer in the U.S., working in the parish where I had lived before, passed quickly: my whole focus was on my last year in Italy. Arriving back in Rome in September of 1986, I felt agitated: what I would do with my life was to be decided by the faculty at the North American College, and I had no guarantee that I would be approved for ordination. I hated the fact that my future was in the hands of others, that I would not be able to decide what work I would do, how or where I would live.

It was sad to return to Rome knowing that this was my last year. Rome had become my home. My visits to California were often unhappy ones. Would it be different when I moved back permanently, as a priest? When I was six years old my parents had moved to a new house in a new neighborhood. Now I had the same feeling: comfort with the present, fear and unwillingness to take a new step. Both then and now I had no control.

I had shaved my beard the previous year, and now I grew it out again, to remind the faculty that I was not conservative. I had to present a new image if I was going to make it through evaluations in November. "Image is everything from now until November," I told Jim. November was approaching fast. The ordination decision had to be made early in the year because of the long preparation process necessary for an overseas ordination. "Well," Jim said, "once you're approved you can tell them to stick it."

This year would be a balancing act: I would have to convince the faculty to approve me for ordination, begin and complete my masters thesis and prepare myself for the changes in my life that would occur in the next nine months.

I still resented going to the Psychological Center, but I had to admit that I had begun to learn things about myself and it was actually becoming a positive experience. That didn't stop me from complaining about it, though. If I'm approved for ordination in November, I thought, then I'll just stop going. The biggest difficulty about the counseling had been finding the time to go there twice a week. It was CF that had become my primary refuge.

It was still warm and we had a loose daily schedule before school started. One morning Jim slipped into my room and said, "I have to tell you about this beach I went to yesterday." I was interested; it was hot enough to swim and I hadn't been to any European beach. "It's a nude beach," Jim went on, "and there are hundreds of naked people there, especially men. Then there are these bushes in the back where all kinds of things happen."

I was shocked on the surface, but intrigued on the inside. "I would never go there!" I said, with a gasp. But that very next week I found myself on the Metro, going out to investigate this beach near Ostia, outside Rome. I was driven not only by curiosity but also by desire that I dared not act out. But, I thought, I was only going there to look.

I didn't know quite where to go. After getting off the bus I walked for hours until I saw the first naked body. I kept walking and there were others, almost all men. I sat and watched the sunbathers. They were lying down, taking walks, playing volleyball, chatting, not self-conscious at all. I was fascinated by the scene. As the sun was setting, I got on the bus and left, resolving never to return. My curiosity had been satisfied.

Somehow the next week I found myself on the same Metro heading out to the same beach. There were hundreds of people there looking for suntans or sex, or both. Many of them went to the brush and coverings in the back seeking out others with similar desires. I sat and walked and watched. I dared not speak with anyone. I had to be careful; Jim had warned me that others from NAC were regular visitors here. Once I had seen enough, I got back on the bus, resolving once more never to return.

Again and again I returned, always resolving not to, feeling guilty that I had gone to such a place. At the fifth visit to this beach, I had my first sexual experience. It was spontaneous, brief, and frightening. At its conclusion I practically ran in a panic from the beach to the bus. I felt dirty, guilty; I needed to be cleansed, to go to confession, to take a shower, to rid myself of this and put it in my past for good. I was also afraid that I might have contracted a disease.

A few days later I met with Father Manning, the priest who was my spiritual director at the NAC. He said, "I thought it a bit unusual, Mark, that you had never brought up sexuality before this, but I figured when you were ready to talk about it you would. I thought there was probably some underlying reason."

I trusted him more than the other priests at the NAC. He seemed more spiritual than the others, not concerned with Church politics. I blurted out, "What if I get sick, get AIDS; what will happen to me?" When I described exactly what I had done, he said, "There's no way you could have contracted AIDS or anything else. You cannot get it just from kissing someone." That was a relief. But what about my other concern: "Does this mean that I'm gay?" I asked, hoping for a negative answer. He asked me if I disliked women.

"No," I said, "not at all."

"Then you're not gay. Don't worry about that."

So this was all a fluke, a repressed sexuality bursting to the surface. It simply meant that I needed to talk about and deal with my sexuality more openly, that was the way to avoid this kind of behavior in the future. I'm not gay, I thought, since I'm not anti-woman, so I don't have to worry about it.

Father Manning had given me some peace of mind and I was relieved; I felt more hope about my path. But a few weeks later, I found myself on the Metro once more, heading out to the beach in Ostia. It was a routine that would play out again and again: sexual activity, back to Rome with guilt and regrets, confession at the Vatican where it was anonymous, and then putting the whole experience behind me forever . . . until the following week.

I knew it was risky behavior: I could be seen by someone at NAC and word would get around. I was also in emotional turmoil because this activity was not compatible with the commitment to celibacy I was going to make the following year. And yet I couldn't resist, it was so appealing. I continued to go until the weather changed and the busses stopped running there. At that point I focused again on my studies, my life at NAC, and especially on Communion and Freedom.

School soon began and I had fewer classes: this was the year to write the thesis. The young American professor I chose to be my thesis mentor turned out to be too busy to meet with me much, so I had to work mostly on my own. I spent many hours on the computer every day, making draft after draft. I had been interested in new developments in theology coming from Eastern Europe, especially from Lublin University in Poland; several professors at the Marriage Institute were from there. In my thesis I wanted to investigate an evolution in theological thought, as well as in Church teaching, on sexuality. I investigated a "theology of the body," in which physical acts "speak" with meaning. This was a step beyond an older conception of natural law. I began to read Lublin theologians, and especially the writings of John Paul II. I found I enjoyed the world of research. Time passed quickly and November soon arrived.

I didn't know the exact day when the decision would be made on my ordination, but I was less nervous than I had expected to be. After so many years, reaching ordination was no longer in my hands and whatever was meant to happen would happen. My life had already taken so many twists and turns, had changed directions in ways I would have been unwilling to go had it been up to me. Yet things had improved, the changes I did not plan had been important milestones for which I was now grateful. This would be the same.

Toward the middle of November, I was called to the seminary conference room. Father Donnel said, "Mark, after meeting with the other faculty members, we have decided to approve your ordination to the priesthood. We would encourage you, however, to continue to integrate yourself into this community and to go to the Psychological Center. We also want to commend you for participating in the folk group and other house activities."

He spoke like a robot. He didn't seem happy with what he was saying. He couldn't vote on the committee because he was my advisor. "Congratulations," he said, with the same stone face. I shook his hand and left. A weight had been lifted. This approval gave me a certain amount of freedom that could not be withdrawn now, except by my bishop, and that simply would not happen. I was free. Once in my room I sat down and looked out the window. I was excited. This year would be different. I could finally enjoy myself. I would no longer have to fear what the faculty thought about me, I no longer had to play political games. As long as I didn't do anything horrendous, my ordination was secure.

———

At the CF meeting the following week, Giovanni told me that during Christmas vacation there would be a trip to the Holy Land organized by a priest of the movement. "I want to go," Giovanni said, "but I don't have the money. Perhaps you could go?"

I had taken out a student loan and actually had $3,000 to help with my final year in Rome. It was more money than I had ever had at any one time. Giovanni explained that the purpose of the trip was not only to see ruins and monuments, but to visit the living communities there: Christian, Jewish and Muslim. "There's a CF community in Bethlehem that the group will spend time with," he added. It sounded like the ideal way to spend my last Christmas vacation.

"You know, Giovanni," I said, "I think I will go."

———

In Jerusalem I was in a completely different world: music, architecture, landscape, flora, food, all like nothing I had experienced before. The tour had been planned to allow us as full immersion as possible into local life. We were booked into Christian Arab hotels to support that struggling community. A seminarian named Charles and I were the only two Americans in our group. The others were Italians, mostly Neapolitan. We began to explore the city as soon as we arrived. Father Nicola, our organizer, wanted us to meet the local people and also to visit those Biblical sites which were archeologically authentic.

In Jerusalem we met the Latin Patriarch, visited with local Jews and Christians and spent time in the Church of the Holy Sepulcher. The guide explained that the church was actually built over an ancient quarry; this provided some archeological support for the Biblical account, which describes the place where Jesus was laid to rest as a new tomb where no one had ever been buried before.

We went to Nazareth where a new basilica had been built. This beautiful town seemed much as it must have been in the time of Christ, set among hills, with small houses, many trees and flowers. Below the basilica is an archeological dig where remains of houses from the time of Christ were found. The church is built over the traditional site of the house where Jesus grew up. We took a boat to Tiberius and sat near the shore at the place where Christ, seated on a rock, asked Peter three times, "Do you love me?" That rock is now partly submerged in the Sea of Galilee. "Do you love me?" resonated with me, for I had struggled with that question. Did I love Christ? Did I love myself? Did I love others? Or were my experiences not love at all but rather something unhealthy and dependent? I didn't know. In this place Peter, too, struggled to answer.

Nearby we visited an archeological dig of an ancient home with an inner room containing graffiti referring to Christ and Peter. Fishing gear had also been excavated at the site, and the entire structure was surrounded by the ruins of a Byzantine basilica. I wondered whether I could be standing in the house of Peter the Apostle, where Christ stayed and slept and ate, as the townspeople gathered outside? Being in that place made Christ seem closer, more real, not in the miraculous sense that so many at San Vittorino had sought, but in an historical way that I found more fascinating.

The last place we visited was Bethlehem. Moved and emotional, I told Charles, my American companion, that what was so amazing to me about being here was that it was so evident that all this really happened! I had always thought of faith as something you experience inside yourself. But here it translated into history. Christ was really born here, he walked here, talked there, lived in that town! Peter had a little house in Capharnaum and I was in the bedroom! I asked Charles, "Can you believe that? Faith seems more real, rooted in history, not divorced from it. It's amazing that history is so alive in this place! It makes you feel like you're part of it!" Charles nodded, but I could tell he didn't feel what I felt.

As we were bussed from place to place I often sat next to Father Mariano, a CF priest from Naples. We found ourselves sharing our understanding of faith and life. Deep in conversation one day on the bus, I asked him: "Could it be that Christ doesn't just put up with our sin, but actually reveals himself through it?" I was thinking of my own human yearnings, sometimes expressed through sexuality. Perhaps my weakness longed for a greater Presence, my inability to reform myself could lead me to seek One who could transform me.

"Yes, yes, that's true," he said. "That is so true that I cannot put it any other way myself." He seemed to understand exactly what I was struggling to say. Even my sexual experiences could have a purpose: they could lead me to seek to be changed by Another.

I began to seek out Fr. Mariano's company whenever I could, especially on the bus. One evening after dinner, he said he wanted to take a walk with me. We wandered through the winding streets of Jerusalem. It was a December night, but the weather was mild and beautiful.

"There are some things about myself I want to tell you, Mark," he began. "I have lived a life of dissipation for many years. In fact, I have jumped from the bed of one person, to another." He spoke slowly, perhaps because he was not sure how well I understood Italian. "And these persons that I went with . . ." he paused. "These people, well, they weren't always women." He wanted me to know that he was opening a secret part of himself few knew about: he was homosexual and struggled and suffered because of it.

"I understand," I told him, "because I have done similar things." I had never admitted these things outside confession. It was an issue that I had always avoided in my consciousness. But I felt a bond with him. I was glad I told him and afraid at the same time. I was vulnerable and terrified of being exposed. At the end of the evening we hugged. After I returned to my room I wondered, could it be that since I could accept Mariano knowing *his* secret, I might be able to accept myself too?

On New Years Eve our guide brought us up to a lookout point above the moonlit city of Jerusalem. Thousands of stars filled the sky and the full moon danced off the Dome of the Rock. It was a night of magic; we kept warm and talked to pass the few hours left. There were some Palestinian youths nearby, awaiting midnight, talking and laughing. Soon Israeli police came and told them to leave, I couldn't understand why.

In any case, I wanted this to be the most special year of my life as I looked upon the glowing city of Jerusalem. "*Mezzanotte!* It is midnight!" someone cried. We all kissed and hugged one another. Father Mariano and I embraced firmly, knowing that a new and important friendship had begun in Jerusalem. I had the impression that he looked at me in a new way that night, a look of affection that was not there before.

Returning to Rome, I found myself feeling out of sorts; the trip to the Holy Land had changed me in a way I didn't understand. It was an experience I longed to hold onto and others on the tour felt the same way. Father Nicola proposed we all meet occasionally to share our experiences.

My buried emotional desires had begun to bubble to the surface once more. This time Father Mariano was their object. In the weeks that followed, I tried to telephone him often but he was seldom at his residence. The few times he called back I was not in my room. Eventually I grew so desperate to hear from him that I stayed in my room day and evening waiting for his call. When the phone rang my heart jumped, but it was never for me. I was miserable. That unresolved need, buried deep within, had stirred to life once more.

Finally he did telephone. "Mark, how are you? I'm so sorry I haven't been able to call you before this. I've been so busy here at the parish. The group that went to the Holy Land is going to meet here in two weeks. Why don't you come down for it? You can stay here." My heart leapt. I accepted.

Misery and joy, sadness and happiness; perhaps Plato was correct when he said that the one cannot exist without the other. The anticipation of seeing Mariano filled me with joyous expectation, but his absence made me suffer. Why? I had known this man for only ten days; I was ignorant of his previous life. In many ways he was a stranger. Nevertheless

I was convinced that our bond was something great, part of God's plan still to unfold. I wasn't yet able to tell the difference between an authentic love, springing from an embrace of one-self and the other, and a co-dependency, in which one is filling one's own deficiency. The first brings peace; the second, only inner strife. My relationship with Amadeo had shown me that. Mariano was different, I thought. My friendship with him will show me how to deal with my sexuality, how to love myself and others in a healthier way. That is what I told myself.

Soon the day arrived and I slipped out of NAC for an over-night, confident that my absence wouldn't be noticed. As the train chugged south, I thought how good it would be to see every-one from the Holy Land, to relive the experience we had shared. I was especially excited about Father Mariano, convinced that our friendship would be something very important to us. Per-haps we could help each other to a greater experience of faith, supporting each other to live the vows of the priesthood, giving each other emotional support to help us keep our sexuality in check. These were my thoughts as I arrived at the parish house. When I met Father Nicola outside I was disappointed to find out that only four others were able to attend. Father Mariano had pasta waiting as we all entered the house and embraced.

We talked over dinner, and Father Nicola said he intended to return to Bethlehem to help those in the CF Movement there. He asked us to consider going there with him. To me, this seemed like an outlandish idea.

"It's late, we are all tired. Mark, where are you staying?" Father Nicola asked.

Father Mariano answered for me. "He has the guest room here."

When the others left, Mariano began to pursue me sexually. I was surprised. I had imagined our friendship would be a way of giving each other emotional fulfillment to avoid acting out sexually. His idea of our relationship was obviously different from mine. In the end I accepted his advances.

Afterward, he was torn by guilt: He said, "We must never do this again. We have to be careful about being alone together." He was completely distraught. I was not as torn by guilt as he was, since to me our friendship was not about sex and would not be reduced to it. The next morning he continued to voice his remorse. I had to go back to Rome. "We'll keep building our friendship and help each other," I reassured him and myself.

I wondered whether Father Mariano had planned this sexual encounter when he asked me to stay with him. Perhaps his excessive guilt revealed a pattern; maybe I was simply one in a series. Was he taking advantage of his position for his physical gratification? I quickly brushed these doubts aside; I was certain that Mariano valued me for myself, certain that he felt toward me as I felt toward him. I had so little experience that I equated sex with love, physicality with affection.

On the train going back to Rome I reflected on the weekend's experience and, as if a spell had been cast, suddenly new and more intense feelings for him blanketed me. It was as if, in a split second, I fell in love (or at least what I thought was love). It came unexpectedly. Although I had felt desire for him before, this was more consuming. It was overwhelming, as if I were on a tightrope, halfway between despair and hope. I wished I could take the next train back to him, but of course I couldn't.

I wanted to believe that my meeting and relationship with Father Mariano were part of God's plan. But as in the past, I wondered how one could discern God's will from the complexity of human needs? I wanted to believe that my desires were part of God's design; that somehow love for another would not take away from, but would actually lead to, the experience of His presence. In the past this had led me to a dead end: I had almost fallen apart over Amadeo. But Mariano was different, I told myself. For so long I had not allowed my heart to love at all; now it was gushing forth. Didn't Thomas Aquinas write that emotions in themselves are neither good nor evil; that what gives them a moral character is how one uses them? I wanted to see my attachment to Mariano as something wholesome, purposeful, and part of a plan for me. But I was still confused: if this was God's will, why was my heart in such turmoil?

Need, both emotional and sexual, came to the surface as the new year began in that final period in Rome. Rather than see these things as a crisis, however, I hoped that they would serve a purpose. I had abandoned a devotional experience of spirituality to take the human road. Within the experience of the Communion and Freedom Movement, I was coming to see that my humanity must play a role in my relationship to God, to Christ. CF held that human desire was to be acknowledged. The great human desires for love, truth and fulfillment must constitute a road. If He is the answer, then my life must somehow be a question. My inability to live up to my own ideals, therefore, could also be this way to a more authentic and human faith.

After being with Fr. Mariano, it was as if I could "feel" more in all of my relationships. Even praying became a more emotional experience. I could not yet see where this awakening within my spirit would lead, but surely it must not be a terrible thing. I would rather be fully alive than half dead, and faithfulness to the Infinite One had to mean life, not death. That was how I tried to make sense of my conflicting feelings.

CF had become my path. When Giovanni asked me to participate in a three-day retreat in Rimini with 15,000 people, I quickly accepted. To be away for several days I had to get permission from my advisor, Father Donnel.

"The retreat begins on Friday and I will be back on Sunday evening. I don't have school until Tuesday, so it will work out perfectly. And, aside from vacation periods, I've never been away from the college before, this is my first and probably my last time." I tried to convince him, as he sat rigidly behind his desk, frowning at me.

"I can't grant your request to go," he said. "You'll miss the community Mass on Saturday evening and I can't let you miss that. You need to become more a part of this community, so no, you can't go."

I knew that many people, including Donnel himself, often missed the community Mass when they went on weekend trips. I replied angrily, "Well, I'm going!" I tossed the paper on his desk and walked out. What did I care at that point? My ordination was approved and Donnel was only a bothersome gnat.

At the retreat in Rimini it was good to be with my companions from the Roman College, away from the NAC and from pining for Father Mariano. During the conferences, as I listened to the CF founder, Father Guardini, speak to the crowd, I felt embarrassed. His words addressed my experience so directly that I was sure he knew about my emotional struggles and was gearing the talk towards me. As he spoke of our human questions and how they manifest themselves in longings and desires, I stared at the ground. I thought he had heard about my weekend at Mariano's parish and was using it as the basis of his sermon.

I was almost ashamed to comment on his conferences during our break time for fear of revealing that "Yes, it was indeed I whom he was speaking about." Later I realized how ridiculous this suspicion was. He was merely expounding on a human experience so fundamental that he was speaking not only to me but to the person sitting next to me. I did discover a promise that weekend, however: the promise that I could be imperfect and still be embraced by Christ and the community, the promise that my heart had a destiny.

———

Back in Rome, my feeling for Father Mariano remained strong, but I refused to go on making myself miserable over it. I would no longer wait in my room for his phone calls. I had other matters to focus on: it was already March and I needed to complete my masters thesis and get ready for my ordination in June. My parents and my brother and sister were planning to come. That made me happy. For the first time I would be able to share my life in Rome with them. I hoped they would finally understand me.

I struggled to complete my thesis. I was getting little help from my official advisor after months of trying to set up appointments with him. Since my subject was fairly original, involving a new wave of theology coming out of Eastern Europe based on the philosophy of Max Scheller, there were not many publications available. I sought out intellectuals who were writing on the "theology of the body." Rome was a magnet for Catholic thinkers, so I was able to interview several men who pointed me in the right direction. I also sat in on some extra classes at the John Paul II Institute and found a few books and articles to weave together my analysis of an evolution in theology. Preparing the thesis gave my life focus for several months and I had no time for much else. I received no phone calls from Father Mariano.

Warm weather began early that year, and by mid-April it was hot. Before long I found myself on the Metro again, going out to the beach of iniquity. The same cycle of feelings resumed: excitement at the prospect of going, fear of being seen once there, enjoyment of the adventure, guilt at having gone when I was returning on the Metro, resolution never to repeat the experience. I was exploring my sexuality a few months before I was to make the vow of celibacy.

"You've been to the beach again." Jim stared at me, his arms folded, as I came out of the elevator in my flip flops, towel in hand, sand on my legs.

"No, I haven't," I replied. It was difficult for me to admit even to myself what I was doing. Jim slipped into my room and got me to admit that I had gone.

"I just went to the mixed part, not the nude part," I said.

Why was I explaining this? Why was I lying?

"Well, just be careful; lots of NACers are starting to go there too."

At the beginning of May we would complete our final preparation for ordination, promising obedience to our local bishop and perpetual celibacy. The promise of obedience didn't frighten me, but celibacy did, considering my recent track record. I was at the point where I would need to make a choice. If I was to move forward, I had to commit myself to celibacy and stop going to the beach. A few days before this commitment ceremony, I was scheduled to give a homily: the reading was from the Gospel of Luke in which the angel appears to Mary and asks her to become the mother of God. I thought long and hard about that reading and about my life, and when I gave the homily, I spoke about Mary's answer and what it meant for me.

"When the angel appeared to her and asked her to become the mother of the Messiah, Mary had no idea where this road would lead. She could not see the future joys or sorrows; perhaps if she had, her answer would have been different. She could not see whether she would always respond to God's call, whether she would always be faithful, how this adventure might play out. She also did not know what role this Son would play, what response He would receive, what mission he would have. And yet she said yes. Why? Because she realized that the center of her life was not her plans or fidelity or reliance on her own strength. She understood that the center of her life was God's plan, and that was enough.

"When we go upstairs to make the commitment we don't know either what will happen to us, if we will be faithful or not, or where the road will lead. But we place God's plan at the center instead of ourselves, and we know everything will be okay. It is a leap of faith, a trust in one who is in control, an adventure. This is what we are about to embark on, just as Mary did."

I went to the grand chapel at the NAC and made the commitment of obedience and celibacy. I knew that in order to live up to those promises, I could not rely only on myself. I put God's plan at the center of my life instead of my weakness and fear. I wanted to live up to the commitment, and my desire to do that, asking God's help, would have to be enough.

———

My thesis had been approved, my grades were in and I had made my vows. The next event was the deaconate ordination. Now the hustle and bustle began: the preparation for the ordination in Saint Peter's basilica and the arrival of family and friends. The days seemed magical again as in that first year at San Vittorino. The college had arranged tours and activities for the parents to give them a great experience of Rome and to keep them distracted so that those about to be ordained would have time to complete their preparations. I had arranged to take my exams early, but some people were taking theirs even after the ordination.

When my parents arrived, I was very happy to see them; all the wounds of the past seemed to fade away. I had never thought I would be with them in Rome. They stayed in a pleasant hotel reserved for the families. The North American College had arranged that some of our professors would take them on a tour; one was Father Foster, my Latin teacher, who was so passionate for the language that he would always say, "In the end, it all comes down to Latin!" He took them to the Forum and immersed them in ancient Roman history. On another tour they went below St. Peter's to a first-century cemetery, identified as the burial place of St. Peter. My parents were having a great time and I was happy.

My brother Mike and my sister Sue arrived a few days later. They were fresh out of college and couldn't afford a hotel so they stayed in an inexpensive *pensione* near the NAC. It was inconvenient for them because there was a ten o'clock curfew. Their plan was to arrive in Rome and then travel through Europe for ten days, returning in time for the ordination. I hadn't had the opportunity to spend much time with them since I had moved to Rome nine years earlier, so I decided to accompany them on half their European trip, going as far as Slovenia. They would meet me back in Rome two days before the ordination.

Mike and Sue had never traveled in Europe before, so I worried about their being overcharged or Sue's being the object of aggressive Italian men. The week I was with them turned out to be a beautiful time; we were on a strict budget, but we were in Europe, listening to a choir in Salzburg, riding the *vaporetto* in Venice, sipping wine with our cousins in the Slovenian hills. I was sad when the morning arrived that I had to leave. I knew I would see my brother and sister in Rome soon, but I didn't know when or if I would return to Slovenia to see my cousins there again. There were many tears as I said goodbye.

———

Back in Rome, there was a whirlwind of activities: a formal dinner for the parents, final conferences, preparations and telephone calls from friends to let me know they were coming. Father Mariano called a few days before to say he would be at my ordination, but he couldn't stay overnight. I was glad he was coming but had no time to focus exclusively on him.

As the ceremony approached I grew nervous. It was a leap into the future, making a lifelong commitment that I hoped I would keep. I was certainly not perfect, nor had I arrived at complete emotional stability. But I wanted to take that road, that step. It was an adventure, like that first time I had arrived at San Vittorino years before. I had longed for an interesting life back in Modesto and this was simply one more step along that path. I decided not to let my worries disrupt the magic of those final days. I refused to put fear at the center of my life.

The night before the ordination I went to bed early. Half an hour later I received a call from my brother Mike. "Sue and I are at the front gate; we want to take you out for a beer," he said. I laughed; the last thing I wanted to do the night before the ordination was drink. I said, "Why don't you guys come up?" I jumped into some clothes and brought them to the roof of the NAC, with its panoramic view of the whole city. We spent some hours in the starry Roman night chatting and being together on the eve of that day that would change my life. It was good to be here; this was goodness and happiness all rolled into one, I thought, as we listened to the sounds of the city below the stars.

———

The bishop ordaining us was Cardinal Bonner, whom the men at NAC called the "Lady in Waiting." I never understood why, except that he was very pink; his face, his ears, his hands, even his bald head. He greeted us one by one in St. Peter's basilica before the ceremony began. My palms were sweaty; I was nervous but happy. I would make the leap and trust in God to do the rest.

A long procession led us up the center of the church to the altar right under the chair of St. Peter. I looked into the congregation and was happy that my family had been seated in front, and Father Mariano was at the altar nearby. My friends from CF were further back; I couldn't see them. As we lay face down on the floor before the ordination rite I asked all the saints to pray and help me to live up to this great calling. I asked St. Peter, who was so human himself, to pray for me. "Help me to be faithful to this step I am about to take."

"May God bring to completion this work he has begun in you," Cardinal Bonner said.

Within an hour we were deacons, the last step towards the priesthood. There was a great feast back at the NAC for family and friends; my CF community from the Roman College came and celebrated, along with my parents and brother and sister.

Marcus walked up the stairs and shook my hand. "Sorry I'm late, I couldn't make the ceremony," he said. I hadn't noticed that he was not at the ordination. It was disappointing, but I said, "That's okay, come on in." Although he stayed to eat and spend some time with my family, he seemed to feel awkward and out of place. I was surprised that he stayed for several hours, since my contact with him had been so limited in recent years. Father Mariano did not come up to the college, saying he had to return to his parish right away. He had said goodbye in St. Peter's Square. As I sat at the table at the NAC I felt happy. A milestone had been reached. The celebrations would continue for several days until our families left.

Within weeks it would be time to return to the United States. It was a voyage I had made many times, but now the finality was frightening. As I packed up my belongings, I wondered what the future would bring. Would I feel isolated? Would I be able to continue the experience in CF that I had had here in Rome? Would I be happy? Would I be faithful? Father Guardini, the founder of the Communion and Freedom Movement, was coming to Rome and I requested an appointment to speak with him before I left.

We sat down together, and I told Guardini about my fears and doubts. I expected him to tell me not to worry, everything would be all right, and I would then try to quash my fears and move forward. But his response was unexpected: "If things prove too difficult for you there, if you feel isolated," he said, "we will find a way to bring you back." He had not dismissed my apprehension; he had embraced and answered it. I was happy when I left him, knowing that ultimately I would be all right no matter where I found myself. I knew this because I had a sense of belonging and I would not be alone again. Now I was ready to depart. My life in the U.S. would not be cut off from my life in Rome. CF would be that link.

Holding On

——

In 1987 I was starting my diaconate, a year of practicing to be a priest. Deacons are assigned to a parish where they perform various liturgical functions, helping out where and when needed. I knew I had to fully fit into the parish and take on its responsibilities but so much of my heart was still in Italy. I found a local community of CF in Berkeley that could be my reference point and connection to my life in Rome.

The parish pastor welcomed me; he was a soft-spoken man who had always been kind to me and my family. I had known him since I was in high school. There was also a newly ordained Portuguese priest in the parish, Edward, who, I would soon learn, had severe mental problems, and a nun named Sister Sally who seemed to think of herself as a co-pastor. I had resolved to get along with everybody and have a pleasant year.

I commuted every week to Berkeley for the meetings of Communion and Freedom, and some American members of the movement sought me out at the parish. I began to write to Father Mariano twice a week and to call him a few times a month. Writing to him, I seemed to feel his affection and support. Once on the phone, he said, "I am sorry I have not written you back, but the work in the parish is very intense." In fact he hadn't written to me at all, but I wasn't upset because I felt sure of the bond between us.

As young people began to seek me out at the parish, Father Edward, the Portuguese assistant pastor, seemed to become more and more hostile. Obviously he disliked me for some reason. I said good morning to him as I left my room after he had finished celebrating the Sunday Mass. His answer as he walked by me into the kitchen was "Fuck you! Go to hell, you bastard!" I asked the pastor for advice: "Just do your best to get along," was all he could say. I decided not to take the insults to heart since this would be only a ten-month assignment and my life was really not here. When news came a few months later that his father committed suicide, hanging himself in a public park, I came to pity Edward as an unhappy and despairing soul.

The local community of CF was my link with the past, but I missed the deep friendships that I had made in Italy. I kept in touch with Giovanni, Pino and Michele, my community from the Roman College. One evening in November after six months here, I decided it would be a good idea to go to Italy to visit Father Guardini to reconnect with the founder of CF as well as with Father Mariano and my Roman community. I asked for two weeks off, and the pastor agreed. I was excited about the trip and to see those whose friendship had become so much a part of my life.

I left in February, planning to stay no more than two nights in any one place. In Milan, Father Guardini welcomed me warmly, asking, "How is it for you there in America?" I told him about it and invited him to visit our small community. "I will come," he promised. Again I felt embraced and comforted. It was as if I were on a firm rock, encircled by a strong friendship that nothing could move; the bonds that had sustained me in Rome continued to hold. He told me I could call him at any time. I felt this was a privilege: there were tens of thousands in Italy who strained to hear his words whenever he spoke in public; few had any sort of personal relationship with him. He regarded me as a friend. This filled me with gratitude.

Guardini was never aloof. When I met and spoke with him at various times, he seemed to place my welfare above even the growth of the movement he had founded. It was this openness that drew so many people of different cultures and religions to him. His connection to his own fundamental humanity enabled him to relate to others and to have a real interest in them. I saw him as one of those "great souls" like Gandhi or Martin Luther King, who are able to enlarge their horizons, to love more deeply than most of us.

It was rainy, cold and gray as I boarded the train from Milan to Rome where I met my community from the Roman College. I spent several hours with Giovanni, Michele and Pino, telling them about my experience in the parish back in America. "We will come for your ordination, we will find some way," they all promised as we said goodbye at the train station.

I felt excitement and tension as I traveled from Rome to Naples to visit the parish of Father Mariano. The excitement was logical, since I longed to see him. But I was unsure of the source of the tension. My stomach didn't feel right. I remembered my stomach pain in San Vittorino that obviously had signaled unhappiness, but I was not sure what my present stomach problems meant.

In any case I was in his small town once more. Father Mariano met me at the train station, accompanied by another man named Mariano whom he said I had met when I was there before. Two Marianos. The new one, about thirty-five years old, tall, very handsome and solidly built, was a layman. He and Father Mariano had become great friends. I didn't recall meeting this Mariano on a previous visit.

"You'll stay with Mariano while you're here; there's more room for you there," Father Mariano said. I was disappointed. He must have his reasons, I thought, but I had hoped to spend time with him.

"So how are you? How have you been?" Father Mariano asked, as we sat in his rectory office later that afternoon. I told him about my time at the parish, about Father Edward, about my pastor.

"Here are some of your letters; I saved them, I haven't thrown them out." He gestured toward a pile of papers on his desk. I had written him time and again about everything: the CF Movement in Berkeley, my new friends there, my family and my upcoming ordination.

"I don't get much chance to participate in the movement here," he said. "Are there any communities of the movement near you?"

"Yes," I said slowly, "I wrote you many times about that . . ."

I had written him dozens of letters describing my involvement with the local CF. Now I suddenly realized that he had never read them.

"That's good, let's go out to lunch," he said suddenly, perhaps to change the subject. I was stunned.

On the train going back to Rome, I wondered about the bond I had forged, or imagined that I had forged, with Father Mariano. He hadn't read my letters. If I had ever received a letter from him I would have read it over and over again. He never called me. It seemed that it was I who was making all the efforts to build and keep a friendship. Did my love for him blind me to the absence of an equal love for me? Or was my love just a need that resembled love but had nothing to do with it at all? Perhaps it was this need that masked the absence of a mutual affection. Why was I so tense during my visit with him? I had no answers. At least, no answers I was ready to accept.

Some months later. Father Guardini came to visit Modesto. I asked Marco, the Italian CF member in Berkeley, why he was coming. "He is coming, first of all, to see you," Marco said, "and secondly, to help what is beginning to grow here."

During his visit it was difficult for me to think of Guardini as a friend, since friendship implied equality. I felt inferior to him; he was so much further along the path that I had just begun to walk. He seemed to have an understanding of humanity and faith that I could barely intuit, and I was ashamed to let others see my limits and deficiencies. It was this feeling that prevented me from behaving naturally around him. His words, his compassion and his wisdom were astounding. The small community in Modesto and Berkeley clamored to be close to him and to make him as comfortable as possible. I took his visit as another confirmation that the CF Movement would be the key to my developing a unified life.

————

The date of my priestly ordination approached. It would take place in May at the Cathedral, and the first Mass would be held in the parish where I had been working for the past year. Most of the preparation was for the first Mass: I had contacted some members of the local opera company; they would sing Mozart's *Missa Brevis*, and a string quartet would perform at the parish reception. I had to have programs and remembrance cards printed, with parts of the ceremony and information about the ordination. I had brought back cards from Italy with the image of the mosaic of the Madonna in St. Peter's Square to send to the printers; I only had to decide what to put on the back.

I reflected on the past, on my ups and downs and all those events that had led me to this point. The connecting thread was always that search for the one essential thing that St. Peter had expressed at the Sea of Galilee when he met Christ after the Resurrection. I decided to print St. Peter's words: "Lord, you know all things; you know that I love you."

Planning for the ceremony turned into a CF event: members of all the communities from the United States were coming to Modesto. My community from the Roman College in Rome notified me that they were coming. A few days before the ordination, as visitors began pouring into the airport, the parish helped me to organize housing for the hundred or so people.

When Giovanni, Pino, Michele and Andrea arrived, I felt embraced. They had been with me from the beginning in CF. When I had had pneumonia they were the first to visit me. Now they were here, despite great financial sacrifice.

It seemed as if everyone I had ever known was present at the ordination: childhood friends, cousins, companions from Rome, college buddies. The ceremony itself was solemn and magical. I couldn't believe that I was reaching this goal after so many years of preparation.

After it was all over, my friends from CF gathered around and hugged and congratulated me. Then they picked me up and threw me in the air over and over again, cheering. The others stood and watched, asking, "Who are these people?" I was happy, I was exhausted, I had arrived and the CF community was there for me. It was 1988, exactly ten years since I had first entered the seminary in Rome.

Boredom and Longing

———

I WAS STATIONED AT ST. ROSE CHURCH, where Msgr. O'Conner had been pastor for over forty years. It was in a close-knit Hispanic community in a poor section of town. There was also a school. My duties at the parish included saying the daily Mass, teaching Bible classes, and being on call for the pastor when he said things like, "I need you to cover this funeral tonight; I've scheduled it at the same time as a wedding practice." My time was his and I had to be ready to cancel my plans at a moment's notice. I had always liked and respected Msgr. O'Conner, but I found it difficult being on call for him.

I was still in CF with a small group of people in my area of Modesto. I was soon made the leader of the movement, both locally and nationally, and found the role more tiring than nourishing. Many of the female members of the local community called me every day for emotional support. I was asked to intervene in every crisis, and in every moment of doubt and depression. I had not learned boundaries then, so I tried to help in any way I could. My days were not long enough to return all the phone calls I was receiving so I began to make "to do" lists, crossing off each call or task as it was completed. These lists were often three or four pages long. It was exhausting.

Most of my parish work consisted of administering the sacraments. I found it curiously unsatisfying. Those who participated in weddings or funerals were rarely, if ever, interested in the ceremony. More often than not the congregation would not even respond to the prayers, and often the bride or groom or the family of the deceased showed no interest in what I was doing or saying at the altar. When I said, "The Lord be with you," the only response would be silence. I came to hate weddings and funerals. The priest was a prop, like the flowers or the incense. He helped to create an atmosphere, but apparently little else.

Preaching became my passion and I began to prepare my sermons a week or more in advance, reflecting and praying over the readings. I was in a poorly educated area of Modesto, and found that I had to speak simply to be understood. Every Sunday the same people attended and every Sunday as they left, they would say, "Nice homily, Father." Was anybody listening?

"I think," I remarked one day to Marco from Berkeley, "if I said, 'God does not exist, this religious stuff is lies and it's better not to come to church at all,' the same people would come up to me and say 'Nice homily, Father.'"

I preached mostly about human experience, desire, friendship and encountering Christ in a vibrant community. It was possible to live this way here; I had seen it in Rome. But I never knew if anyone got the message. There were times when some young people came to the CF meetings in the parish to see what they were all about. More often than not, they never came back, complaining that too many "big words" were being used.

It wasn't enough for me to sow the seeds; I wanted to see them grow. My own sense of purpose and fulfillment was tied to whether anyone in the parish responded to my message and joined the movement. In Rome such things did not worry me; it was my own path that I was concerned about and the movement there was already mature. Now I was a leader in the parish and in Communion and Freedom. I began to grow frustrated with the lack of response. Was it my fault or theirs? I didn't know.

In addition to my frustrations with seeing no results from my efforts, I was increasingly uncomfortable with being a public person. In the past I had always preferred to be private; I never wanted to be the center of attention. In the seminary there were classes in theology and in counseling, but never in living one's life in the spotlight. One day I received a letter from a pious Catholic woman who wrote, "I saw a photo of you wearing secular pants. I think this is shameful and inappropriate." She was referring to a pair of gray trousers that I sometimes wore with my clerical shirt.

On another occasion, a parishioner came up to me and asked, "Father Mark, are you losing your hair? It seems to be thinning out." A week after that a young man remarked, "Looks like you're dyeing your hair. What kind of a priest would do something like that? Who are you trying to look good for?" And there was the sympathetic question from someone else: "Father, you looked so sad during the Mass; what's wrong?"

I was constantly being deluged with comments about my physical appearance and/or my emotional state. I reached the point that, on my day off, I would just go to my parents' empty house to hide.

Months went by. The rectory where the priests lived was on a busy boulevard and often people would stop by looking mostly for money or sometimes for the blessing of a car or a statue. Since the rectory was on a buzzer system, my day was peppered with the sound of the buzzer calling me to come downstairs and deal with some unexpected demand. The constant buzzing was irritating; I couldn't get any work done in my room. I began to go out on the grounds or in the church to escape the sound or just to have some peace to reflect or pray. When I was in my room one afternoon I was being called so constantly that I ripped the buzzer off the wall. A few days later, the pastor asked me what had happened to the buzzer upstairs. I shrugged and told him I didn't know.

A retired priest, Father Boland, also lived upstairs; he had been a priest for fifty years, and had been living in the rectory for years before I came there. He was a good man and was kind to me. I had known him since I was a child. A few weeks after I came, he fell ill and was taken to the hospital. I was planning to pay him a visit, but in the afternoon the pastor came into the rectory and said that Father Boland had just died of heart failure. "He didn't have any visitors. He passed just as I was walking over to his room. God rest his soul."

I went to my room, feeling depressed. Father Boland had given his life to others, he had been a priest in this city for half a century, in this parish for fifteen years, and he had died alone. "I will not die alone," I said out loud. I would refuse to live my life that way, would refuse to be alone so that when I fell sick and died no one would notice or care.

The CF meeting in my parish became the focal point of my week. Since I was the guide, it was I who was expected to provide insights, to lead the members to new ways of living. With the daily routine in the parish, my public persona and my leadership role, I began to feel more and more exhausted and empty. I was often sick: a cold would turn into an infection with fever and chills. I was taking a cycle of antibiotics twice a month; it seemed that I was well for only a few days before I came down with something else. I had never been fat, but now I lost weight; my clothes were loose. I overheard people saying, "Father Mark is sick again."

Nearly a year passed and my cycle of infections continued. One winter afternoon, as I curled up under my blankets with the chills from a fever, I came to a realization: "If I don't do something about my health, I'll be dead in a few years." I joined a local gym and worked out in the afternoons when the parish quieted down. Joining the gym helped me become aware of my unhealthy lifestyle. Partly because of the parish cook, of which more later, I started to cook my meals myself instead of running out for hamburgers and Mexican food when I was hungry. Within a few months I had gained twenty pounds, mostly muscle, and, almost like a miracle, I no longer got sick.

I began to make friends at the gym with people who didn't know I was a priest, or knew and didn't care. It was refreshing to form friendships based on mutual acceptance instead of on my being a priest or being in CF. I sometimes doubted whether those close to me in the parish or in the movement in Modesto would be friends with me if they really knew me, if I was not playing any role at all. I enjoyed being with my new friends at the gym, and tried to devote time to develop these relationships.

———

In the spring I received a phone call from Italy. I was surprised to hear the voice of Father Mariano. I had not been in contact with him for over a year.

"Mark, how are you?" he asked. "How is your life in the parish?"

I began to fill him in; after a minute or two he interrupted me: "Yes, I called to find out how you are and to make a proposal." I knew I was about to hear the real purpose of his call. "There is a church here which is very poor to the point of not being able to sustain itself. The proposal is this: your parish could be a sister church to this one and they could help sustain each other."

Dismayed, I answered: "That would be very difficult because my church is poor too, but I'll speak to the pastor."

Needless to say, I didn't mention it to the pastor. I was very annoyed that, after all those years, Father Mariano had called me only to ask for money. Why had I been so blind as not to see that it was not a reciprocal love? The door that had opened to Mariano was now shut forever.

The need to love can be confused with love itself. Both are blinding and exceedingly emotional. The need to love, however, is more extreme than real love. It is fed by need and depends on the other for happiness. It is slow to see who the other truly is, since the heart, and not the mind, is its guide. It is need and co-dependency dressed in the clothes of passion, affection and generosity. Love itself is more focused on the other than on oneself, finding its reward in the happiness of that other. Love is more detached than need, yet can be more passionate. Peace is the sign that one truly loves. Need is always restless and insecure. I began to understand these things as I gave up Father Mariano.

———

So much of my time and energy in the parish was spent with people who were already very much involved in the Church that I felt I was "saving the saved." I didn't enjoy working with these deeply pious people. I felt the same way about them as I had toward the very religious seminarians in the Oblates. The more pious they were, the less human they seemed. I longed to be with people who were more involved with life, who were active and had interests, who perhaps were not religious but who thought about the meaning of their existence. I would never meet people like that at St. Rose; I knew I would have to leave the church steps and branch out into the world. Since I had a masters degree, I began to apply for teaching positions at local schools and received and accepted an offer to teach in the philosophy department of a local community college.

The focus of my course was the relation of the thoughts of the great philosophers to one's own existence. I was assigned to teach a unit on the question of God, but I changed the topic to "The Search for Meaning," and used a text by Father Guardini as required reading. It was a great success: students actually stayed after class to discuss the topic. Teaching invigorated me and I began to see a new road. Perhaps after I completed my five-year term in the parish, I could attain the doctorate and find a full-time teaching position. I wanted to be immersed in the world, involved with people who were thinking and searching rather than spending most of my time blessing automobiles and performing weddings for uninterested participants. I began to search for the road that would lead me to full-time teaching.

———

The parish was supposed to have meals prepared for the resident priests, but the pastor didn't want to spend money for a cook so we fended for ourselves. As I mentioned, I ate a lot of junk food. One day the pastor brought in as his personal assistant a young man named Neil, who had been kicked out of the seminary but who had delusions of being a priest. Neil lived in the rectory and often dressed like a priest. He was a troubled man who longed to be an authority figure. His job was to run errands for the pastor and to cook dinner. It was the same meal every day: a chicken breast cooked until it became so dry it was stringy, a microwaved potato and frozen peas.

"Neil, can you make something different some time?" I asked one day. The next night he served me a plate of the same food, but the peas were orange.

"You said you wanted something different, so I cooked the peas in orange Jell-O," he explained.

Since I wasn't sure of his mental state I decided not to challenge him in any way. His presence in the rectory added to my discomfort. Often parishioners addressed him as "Father" and he seemed pleased; he was known to masquerade as a priest and counsel people who came in. But I decided not to fight this battle and simply to concentrate on my own work.

Since I had taken on other responsibilities outside the parish, I had to protect my schedule from the pastor's "crisis management." I needed time to prepare for my classes, to do the readings and correct papers. How could I find that time if the pastor was always calling me to fill in for his bad scheduling? I found that isolating myself was the best way. If I didn't

see him, he couldn't ask me to drop everything and take care
of a forgotten appointment. And as I have said, I decided to
adopt a healthier lifestyle when I joined the gym. So I stopped
showing up for dinner at 5:30 and cooked my own food an
hour or two later.

———

After my first two years in the parish, I connected to the inter-
net because I needed to e-mail the CF leadership in Milan.
But the chat rooms proved irresistible. I found myself spending
hours chatting online and seeking out real sexual experiences.
I was careful not to act out in my town; and often drove dis-
tances for liaisons. This went on for about six months. Obviously I was living a double life: priest and national leader of CF
while sexually active in secret. I couldn't cut ties with my role
or with my sexual needs. I felt trapped. I was in a dangerous
place and I dared not speak of it to anyone.

I wondered about the many friends I had made in CF here
in the U.S. Were they really friends? Did they value me for who
I was or for the role I played? Who really knew who I was? I
presented myself as a strong masculine figure, even making
anti-gay jokes. I still had trouble admitting to myself that I was
homosexual, but I was certainly drawn to men. Many in CF
made very hostile remarks about homosexuals and homosexuality, so I knew that if they ever discovered who I really was,
they would no longer be my friends.

The friendship that was spoken about so often at the CF
meetings began to seem to me superficial, no longer reaching
to my core. In fact, it became a strain. In Italy it had not been
like that; I had no prominent role and was just part of something that was already ongoing. Here I was trying to create a
community based on what I had lived in Rome, but I didn't feel
really part of it. Was my sexuality clouding my feelings and
my judgment? Was it making me doubt my friendships in the

movement? Or was I feeling distant because I hadn't revealed all of myself to these people? I felt bad about my homosexual feelings, bad about my friendships and my role.

There was a chat room out of San Francisco that I sometimes entered and I made contact with a man who asked me to drive over to see him the following evening. I pushed all misgivings aside in the eager anticipation of this encounter. It took hours to drive to his city on a Saturday night. His home was in the Castro district. He asked if I would like to go out for a bite to eat and we walked together to a nearby café. After an hour or so we left the café to go back to his place, and as we walked across the street, I heard a loud voice: "Father Mark, what are you doing here?"

My companion walked on. I stopped in the crosswalk to see a station wagon filled with CF members from the San Francisco community. The man I had met had walked to the other side of the street. I went up to the car, horrified that I had been caught in the gay district.

"What are you guys doing here?" I asked.

"We just came down here to see the faggots," the driver said.

"I came down to see a friend of mine, I'll e-mail you tonight," I said and they drove off.

I took leave of the man I had met, badly shaken. Perhaps the world knew what I was not prepared to admit: that I was gay. Back at the parish, I sent the e-mail to the CF man who was driving that car, telling him that I had come down to speak with a gay high-school friend. I didn't know if they would believe the story; I couldn't control their doubt nor their whispering. I told myself that this had to be my wake-up call: no more trips to meet sexual partners, no more sexual acting-out at all. I endured some teasing about the incident for several weeks but then the issue seemed to subside. Perhaps the veil of privacy was still in place. I hoped so.

———

Let me see, I said to myself sadly in my room in the rectory, how many years do I have left? Forty, maybe forty-five; this isn't a bad way to live out my days. My life had become a burden; I looked forward to the evening so I could go to bed and forget about everything.

As I looked in the mirror the next morning I wondered: who has the say in my life? Who gets to call the shots? In the parish the pastor controlled much of my time, the bishop controlled where I would live. I valued my friends at the gym, but the local leaders of Communion and Freedom cautioned me against having such close friendships with people outside the movement. So I couldn't even choose my own friends. The joy I had experienced in CF had been replaced by a sense of responsibility and there was no one to whom I could open myself up completely without being rejected.

My whole being seemed to be incompatible with the life I was living. Could I cut myself off from my emotions, get rid of my computer that had become a window into sexuality and simply live out the rest of my days as a parish priest? I knew exactly how my future would unfold, what the next forty years or so would bring. I had to accept the routine and be faithful to my commitment.

The only positive experience I had now was teaching philosophy at the local college. I thought this could be my road to a new existence. I looked into American universities that would recognize my degrees from a pontifical university, and found only one: Catholic University in Washington D.C. They had a two-year residence requirement for the doctoral program, after which I could return to Modesto and complete my thesis. Then I could get a teaching position which would give me more freedom and be more interesting than "saving the saved." All I had to do was convince the bishop to pay the tuition and release me from the parish. I didn't think getting the release would be difficult, since my five-year term was up and I was set to be transferred anyway. But being given that amount of time outside the diocese might be tough, because of the shortage of priests.

I had no positive or negative feelings about the bishop, Bishop Cohan; he was the ultimate authority in the local church, so I had to answer to him. He smiled often, and had more lines on his face than a map of Manhattan. I was ushered into his office to make my case.

"At this juncture," I told him, "when my term at St. Rose is up, I would like to attend Catholic University for four semesters to pursue the doctorate in moral theology. Few priests in Modesto have a doctorate, so I think that I could benefit the diocese. And I would come home during the summers so I wouldn't be away for two solid years."

After a pause, he nodded.

"Does that mean yes?" I asked, surprised.

It did. It was like a miracle! But I pushed further. "Also, I would like to stay in the dorms there. There is one exclusively for priests. I'm completely burnt out from parish life and I'd like to focus more on my studies." The norm at Catholic University was for a priest-student to obtain free room and board in exchange for helping out at a parish.

The bishop agreed that I could stay in the dorm on a trial basis. I was overjoyed. I would have some freedom from the constraints of a parish, freedom that I had not had in a long time.

When I told the pastor, he said, "You're better off here at the parish, Mark. But if that's what you want to do, fine." He had always been supportive.

I phoned the news to the CF community in Berkeley, and met with them a few days later. Marco, the Italian leader of the community, told me that it had been decided in Italy that I should live with Father Gerald in Washington. Father Gerald was a CF priest serving in a parish near the city.

I was dumbfounded. I didn't want to live in a parish, I was looking forward to some privacy and freedom, neither of which I would have in that parish with Gerald. At that instant I made a decision to do something I had never done before: deceive the leadership of CF. Until that point I had entrusted my life to the movement, but now I felt I must take it into my own hands. I told them, "The decision about where I am to live isn't totally mine, it's my bishop's. He's decided that I should live in the dorms, to complete my studies sooner."

"Will you ask your bishop to reconsider?" Marco asked.

I said I would, but I never did.

When I got home I looked at myself in the bathroom mirror; this was my "moment of truth" place. Why, I thought, did I have no control over my own life? How did things get to this point? I wanted the freedom to choose, I wanted my own life back. I knew I would have to fight for it.

The Door Opens

———

IN 1993, AFTER HAVING SERVED IN the parish for five years, I arrived in Washington D.C. exhausted from the cross-country drive, but elated to be there. My dorm room was about six by ten feet, with only a bed and a desk. But it was my space and I didn't have to obey anybody's schedule but my own. I could participate in meals or not, I could come in at any time. I was free. For several days I rested, unpacked and explored the city, relishing my anonymity.

On the fifth day I received a phone call from Father Gerald, asking me when I had arrived. When I told him, he wanted to know why I hadn't called him right away when I got in.

I paused to think of acceptable reasons. "I was tired, I've just been resting." In reality, of course, I had simply wanted to enjoy my freedom. How wonderful it had been to walk through the streets, go into a shop and not be recognized as a priest or as the leader of CF.

He asked whether he could come over to see me that afternoon. I said yes, resenting the loss of privacy.

When my classes began, I realized I could tell CF members who wanted me to participate in social events several nights a week, that I had to focus on my studies. It was different during the day, however. Father Gerald came over frequently, often unannounced. It reached the point that I could recognize his step in the corridor and I began to keep my door locked when I was in my room. At times, I simply didn't answer his persistent knocking. Inevitably he would call later, asking where I had been. I usually told him that I was at the university studying. I resented this intrusion and the demand for accountability.

The CF community in Washington were life-long practicing Catholics who tended to be on the conservative side, active in the pro-life movement and the Republican party. Some were trying to become more open through CF, but I found no one there with whom I could bond, and when they spoke of friendship in the weekly meetings, my heart felt empty. But I kept going to the meetings out of a sense of responsibility and the fading memory of my experience in Rome.

———

My life settled into a routine, with classes, homework and the CF meeting, but I wanted more. I kept my Fridays and Saturdays free and began to go out into the city. I frequented clubs and bars and simply watched and listened. I didn't know how to relate to a world that had been no part of my own. I began to explore the city sexually also, hiding the fact that I was a priest. I started to have fun enjoying the freedom. I pushed any guilt to the back of my mind; this was my time to explore and I wanted to make the most of it.

More sexual and emotional feelings began to surface during those days and weeks. Once more I was walking a tightrope between hope and despair. It was a precarious state and I felt afraid. The old feelings that had surfaced with Amadeo, and then with Mariano, were pushing to the surface again. It was time to confront them so that they wouldn't take over my life again. I sought help, and found a therapist recommended by a friend at Catholic University.

For the first time I found myself talking about events and emotions that I had either dismissed as unimportant or dared not reflect on.

"Mark," the counselor said one day, "I want you to tell me about your mother: who she was, her sickness, and how she died." I had never shared this with anyone and I felt awkward.

"Did you cry at her funeral?" he asked.

"No, I didn't."

"Weren't you sad?"

"Of course. I don't know why I didn't cry."

"How long has it been since you cried?"

"I can't remember. Years. I have no memory of when I cried last or why." I told him about my mother's cancer, her suffering and death. That afternoon I wept for her for the first time and continued to weep for several days.

"I had forgotten how to feel, but if it's like this all the time I would rather not feel at all," I told him one day.

"That's how you've lived most of your life. But sadness is just the other side of happiness. Why don't you try a different way now," he suggested.

A release valve was opening in my emotional life that I didn't yet know how to control. Even though I was afraid of my emotional turmoil, I could glimpse the possibility of happiness.

———

Months passed and soon it was Christmas vacation. I flew home to California for three weeks. When Don, from the local CF community, asked me about my time in D.C., I didn't know what to say. I suddenly felt like a foreigner, far from those with whom I had shared my life. So much had changed: I no longer understood who I was and there had been a complete transformation in my goals. "Fine. It's going great. The classes are great," I answered finally.

I concelebrated the Christmas Midnight Mass at St. Rose, feeling strangely out of place in my priestly robes. After two days I realized that Modesto was no longer home; Washington was where I belonged, where I was coming alive. Here there were only empty forms, like molds that I had to press myself into so that I could function. There I could continue becoming a whole person.

The next day I went to the cemetery to visit my mother's grave. "Mom," I pleaded through tears, "help me to find the way to happiness. All this time I have tried to do God's will. Is it His will that I return and go on the way I did in the parish in Modesto, unhappy and starting to live a double life? Can I live a life consistent with my promises? Or is there a new path I need to follow, back in D.C.? Help me to find the answer!"

The day after that, I told my father, "Dad, I'm going to return to D.C. early. There's a flight this Friday. I want to get back earlier to get ahead in my studies."

The real reason had nothing to do with my studies. I felt uncomfortable here where the people I knew related to the Mark who was before, not the new Mark, the one who was changing so quickly. Since God works through real people and things, I didn't see any of these changes or events as evil or against His will. Could it be He who was leading me through these new adventures? Could this be His will for me? My prayer at my mother's grave urged me forward.

Coming back to D.C. was like arriving home. I had made new friends who were in no way connected to CF and who didn't know that I was a priest. As I continued to grow and make my own choices without pressure from others, I became increasingly uncomfortable with the role of national leader of the Communion and Freedom Movement. I had moved out of the student dorm and into an apartment that my bishop had agreed to pay for because it was cheaper. I began to taste more freedom and then to hunger for it. My life as national leader was often under a microscope and I was tired of accounting for my time and affections.

I had also decided that I was homosexual, and I became more sensitive to the homophobic remarks so common among the CF leadership. I felt I was cast in a mold that no longer fit. I needed to get out, to leave the leadership position. I wanted a more private life. A national CF meeting was planned for late January and I knew I had to find the strength within myself to resign as leader and keep my own issues private.

To make a difficult decision for one's life requires great strength and often it is easier to seek this strength from others. Self-doubt undermines decision-making and prevents one from moving forward. I knew I had to search for the strength within myself, because the whole CF leadership, especially the Italians, would never understand or support such a radical change. Certainly they would want a full explanation of how I had reached that decision. I had come to believe that God was touching my life through the community I had discovered in CF. But couldn't He lead me in other ways, through other people and circumstances? Could my new friends and life experiences be part of that Divine plan and not a falling away from it? That seemed reasonable to me.

Some weeks before the national CF meeting I told the Italian leadership my intention to resign. I wanted to give them time to find a new leader. The backlash was alarming. My phone started ringing off the hook to the point that I let the answering machine pick up all the calls. Meetings with me were set up and I was told that I must go to Italy to speak with Father Guardini as soon as could be arranged. I did not want to go to any meetings or defend my decision to anyone. I just wanted to slip quietly aside. But I didn't know how to refuse any of these demands for meetings and explanations. My sense of duty and obligation was so strong that I felt like a slave. I wanted to be free, but I didn't know how.

Silvano, a CF representative from Milan, demanded, "This decision of yours was made completely on your own, not with the community. Can you explain to me why, leaving out no details?"

I knew that the CF network often passed around delicate information about its members, so of course I wasn't willing to divulge my personal issues and struggles to him. When he insisted, I said, "Some things are better left between me and my priest in confession." I was making a final attempt to defend the wall of privacy I had begun to build around my life. I felt I was establishing a place where I could find myself.

"The road you are choosing is full of errors and pitfalls; you can avoid these if you stay with us," Silvano insisted.

I paused and said, "If I make mistakes, they'll be my mistakes. I want to be able even to make my own errors, Silvano."

"Okay," he said, giving up for the moment. "I won't push you any further."

This was the first of many battles that I had to fight to get my life back. I had given it away, piece by piece, and no one wanted to hand it back without a struggle. I looked around for support, and found Tony, a friend I had met in the gym years before, and Ron, a priest from Brooklyn whom I trusted. I had told him my situation in the strictest confidence, and he had agreed that I should not be national leader because it put too much pressure on me.

These were the first words of encouragement I received. But what I needed could not come from friends or those I loved. This had become the most difficult fight of my life and I had to find the courage to win it within myself. If I lost this battle I would be lost forever. I was depressed but determined to gain my freedom before I left the national meeting. I was told on my arrival that I was to share a room with Silvano—a deliberate tactic, I felt, to break me down. "No," I said, "I already have a roommate. Ron." Fortunately I had already made an arrangement with Ron to share a private space.

Silvano approached me outside. "You don't have to go to Italy to see Father Guardini if you don't want to," he said. "It's not necessary. Father Guardini said that the most important thing is to respect your freedom." Was I winning the fight?

This was perhaps the most difficult weekend I had ever spent. I resigned my leadership role, while trying at the same time to keep my private life to myself. When I was asked to preach at the final Mass, I decided to tell them exactly what I was feeling.

"Christ can intervene in our lives in the ways and through the people that He chooses," I said, thinking of my life over the past seven months. "Usually they are not people or circumstances that we would have chosen ourselves. Usually He uses the unexpected circumstances to lead us to a greater life, never the one we planned. We just need to be open to His ways and the times that He chooses to shake up everything."

Later that day at the meeting, I said calmly, "I need to focus more on my studies, so Andrew will take on the responsibilities of national leader at this time." It was a simple statement that changed everything. As I left the meeting I noticed the concern and anxiety on the faces of the Italian leadership, but I was overjoyed. It was a milestone, I had taken one step toward repossessing my life. I didn't yet realize that liberation feeds upon itself and seeks an increase just as happiness does.

"You will continue to come to the CF leadership meetings in New York, of course," one of the Italian leaders prodded me. I gave a noncommittal answer.

But when I returned to Washington, not only did I refrain from participating in the leadership, I stopped going to the weekly CF meetings as well. I was letting go of my attachment to that movement which had been an essential part of my being up to that point. The cord that had connected my life in America with Rome seemed to have been severed. It was not a well-thought-out decision: it came out of necessity. I could no longer associate with people who had known the old Mark, who expected me to act and think in a certain way. I was able to make this break because I knew I had to move forward. I was convinced that God was still with me; He was still guiding me. I couldn't believe that I was abandoned as I sought a truer path.

My counselor in Washington asked me when I had been happiest. My answer was simple, immediate and clear. "When I felt most free."

"That happiness that you felt at different moments, how would it be if you could experience it your *whole* life, *every* day? How would that be for you?" he asked.

I thought for a moment. "If I could, that's how I would live. I would want that sense of freedom for my whole life. But how? I'm free of the CF leadership, but I'm still a priest, still under obedience to my bishop, still under all the obligations of being a priest."

He pressed further: "Would you ever consider leaving the priesthood?"

I was shocked. "How could I? I think it was God's will that I became a priest. How could I leave? And I've always identified the Church with the hierarchy, so that obeying the Pope and bishops is obeying God's will. Leaving the priesthood would be like a betrayal, going against God."

"Mark, I want you to think about something: why can't it be that the same God who called you into the seminary to do His work is now calling you out of the priesthood to continue to do His work? Perhaps His presence is not reducible to the institution of the Church; maybe it's both greater and more personal than that. I don't want you to answer, I just want you to think about these things."

But did I dare to think the unthinkable?

I called my friend Tony back in California and, with great effort, revealed my struggle. I didn't understand how my sexuality could be compatible with my faith. If I was gay, how could I be a good Catholic or Christian? The Church had been and still was my life. Did I have to choose one or the other?

Tony said, "You have to resolve your feelings about your sexuality *before* you compare it with the Scriptures or the Church. First you have to be at peace with yourself, before you can find where you fit in God's plan."

His meaning was not clear to me, but I reflected on it for weeks. I slowly realized that up until now I had invented the person I wanted to be and it was this imaginary person that I presented to form relationships with others and with God. This was the source of my difficulty. I decided that the first step would be truth; I must be true to myself before I could be true to others and to God. I am the person I am. Part of who I am is a result of my or others' actions, other parts are biological and from the Creator. Whether by primary or secondary causes, I am this person. God formed me to be who I am, directly or through life's circumstances. What I cannot change about myself must be good, it must come from Him. I will be true to myself, I will no longer hide or fear who I am. My friendships will be based on truth from now on. I began to pray for the first time: "God, thank you for making me who I am, thank you for your work in me." If I am made in His image I must learn to love myself as He does. I had already learned how easy it is to hate oneself.

Self-acceptance led to a gradual re-evaluation of my place in the world and in the Church. I had never felt alienated from the Church and I did not feel that way now, even though my lifestyle conflicted with its sexual teachings. I could only understand this by starting, not with the teachings but with more essential and direct evidence: myself. I am who I am through few choices of my own. Part of who I am is that I am gay, which encompasses not only my sexuality but my way of looking at the world and of relating to everything. God had to have made me this way, whether directly or through circumstances. He must be pleased with me, He must love me for who I am. That is how I found peace with myself and with God. I didn't understand how all the teachings of the Catholic Church applied to me but I didn't feel that I needed to understand. I would continue to be true to myself and to participate in the life of the Church that held so much meaning for me. All other judgments I would leave to God.

———

Even at the beginning of the second semester at Catholic University, my mind was already focused on the summer. I was scheduled to return to the parish in Modesto for three or four months after my exams in May. That was something I didn't want to do. It would be like moving backward into a life that no longer seemed to be mine. The bishop, my pastor, the movement, all had taken chunks out of my ability to choose for myself until there had been nothing left. When I left the leadership of the movement, the feeling was exhilarating. "I want to make my own choices and make my own mistakes," I had told Silvano. I recalled my own words again: "I might make mistakes, but they will be my mistakes, my road, my life."

Could I stay in D.C. and not return home? I hated the thought of going to Modesto and playing out a role that was now alien to me. I wrote to my bishop asking that I remain to take summer school classes and begin research into my thesis topic. This seemed to be a plausible reason why he should let me stay.

I reflected again and again on the words of the counselor: dare I think of leaving the priesthood? In my whole life I had felt and acted as the victim of my circumstances, obeying those who had some power over me. I had never seen myself as having any ability to control my life or my destiny, but rather as one who passively accepted what I was given. That year in D.C. this began to change. Just as the protagonist of a novel is the center of the action, I too could choose to be that central figure in this story of my life, no matter how daunting the obstacles.

An insight came to me as I stood waiting for the subway near the Catholic University: the icy wind was whipping through my coat and I was cowering, crunched over, trying to protect myself against nature's forces. "Wait a minute, Mark," I said to myself, "don't be the victim, not even here. Don't cower. The wind is cold; stand up straight, face into it! Don't let it determine your posture or your behavior. You be in control, not it!" and I stood up straight. From that day forward, "Don't be the victim" became my silent mantra. Another chapter of my life was closing; a new one was beginning.

Several weeks later a letter arrived from the bishop ordering me to return to the diocese as soon as classes ended, and to work in a parish that summer. I repeated my mantra and made a decision within five minutes of reading his letter. I would not go back. Would I leave the priesthood? Such a drastic step frightened me. I quickly wrote out a response: "Your Excellency, I have decided to take a leave of absence from the diocese for a period of time and so am unable to return to Modesto in May."

I was not leaving the priesthood *per se*, I was distancing myself. But how would I survive financially? I contacted a former housemate from the university and asked him about a large non-profit organization that he had told me was hiring.

"Sure," he said. "You want a job? I can set it up for you."

Soon I had a guarantee of employment. Things were beginning to move more quickly: the slow train of my life became a roller coaster.

Several weeks later the bishop wrote back to tell me, "The decision to go on a leave of absence is not yours, but ours. You are to return to the diocese immediately; if you do not I will suspend you."

At about the same time my medical bills for counseling were refused by my insurance company. Apparently the diocese had cancelled my medical insurance at the first sign of trouble. I repeated my mantra once more in answering the bishop's letter. "Bishop, just as you must follow your conscience and do what you believe is right, I must do the same. I am not returning to Modesto this summer and I am taking a leave of absence from the diocese." In effect I was leaving the priesthood, a step I had never thought I would or could take.

I began to get phone calls at all hours of the day and night. It was largely the Italians from the movement who were calling; they wanted to come see me, to influence me to return to the fold. That pressure drove me further away. The last straw was a message from Italy on my answering machine: "Marco, this is your old friend Father Mariano. I am calling to see how you have been and how you are and to speak with you. Please call me back as soon as you get this message."

They had even tracked down Father Mariano to call me; it seemed there was no tactic they wouldn't try. Obviously I had to get away— move to another part of the city, change my phone number, disappear.

———

I was finally free; anonymous in a busy part of the city, working for a non-profit organization, earning enough to survive. I was in control of my life. I kept my unlisted phone number and rejoiced in the privacy of the house that I was renting. I was beginning an entirely new existence completely disconnected from my former one, except that I still practiced my faith. The difference was that my religious experience had become private and I avoided anyone at the church who tried to talk to me.

I was afraid of my past and terrified of even seeing someone from the CF community. I wouldn't know what to say. At times, when I thought I spied someone on the street from the movement, my heart would leap in terror and I would hurry in the opposite direction. Why was I so afraid? I had completely disconnected myself from my past life and I didn't know how to relate to it. I didn't want anyone in my new life to know about my life in Rome or the priesthood. Since I had no idea of how to reconcile my past and present, it was easier to try not to think about it. I cut off all contact with anyone whom I had known before I left except for my family. And even with them I kept communication to a minimum.

But despite all these fears I was happy. The freedom to make choices, whether trivial or life-changing ones, filled me with joy. I had never had such freedom before and I thanked God every day for giving me the chance to live a totally new life. I eventually bought a house on Capitol Hill and planned to settle there.

The unexpected can often be better than what's planned. I had learned this from past events and that was to prove true once again. Even though I had received several promotions, I realized that I needed to have a sense of purpose and to find meaning in my work. I felt drawn to the teaching profession. It would be a way to make a difference in other peoples' lives and, if I taught history, I could put my knowledge and experience from Europe to use. Less than a year after I bought my house, I got an offer for a teaching job in Los Angeles.

"I don't think you should go to California, at least not now," my friend Vincent said. "You just bought a home, you're moving up at work. Are you going to just give all that up to move?" His objection was certainly reasonable, but it made no sense to me at all at the time.

"Vincent," I said, " I have to be happy, happier than I am now. I don't want to live with regrets; I don't want to wake up when I'm sixty and regret not having changed paths when I had the chance. Now is my chance."

The thought of embarking on a new path back in California filled me with joy until a few days before leaving. When my friends came to say goodbye I felt sad and exhilarated at the same time. I had grown attached to my life in Washington and assumed that I would stay for many years. My friends there were my family, and I hated to leave them. At the same time I was excited because I was putting my happiness first, before anything else. My future was once again full of uncertainty but I was free and wanted to use my freedom to build something positive and fulfilling.

The Path Unfolds

———

I HAD FEW FRIENDS FROM MY past when I moved back to California in 1996, since, as I have said, in Washington I had had no contact with anyone outside my family who had known me as a priest or as a member of CF. As a result, in California my former close friends were now strangers. I thought they would consider my leaving to be a betrayal. Perhaps I had caused a scandal. Had I harmed the faith of others? I didn't know and I didn't want to know. That would be an unfortunate but unavoidable consequence of my choices.

Eventually my fear of encountering someone from my past began to recede. My life in Rome and my life as a priest were part of who I was. Some of my co-workers did know about my past and that was not as terrifying as I had expected it to be. I still didn't want to be seen as a former priest or anything else. I was a person, not a role, and I would not let myself fall into being treated that way again.

I felt fulfilled in my new career; it seemed to unify my past and my present. I could actually speak to my students about my European experience instead of hiding it. I was still not completely comfortable with others knowing everything about my past because I wasn't yet at peace with it myself. I still wondered if I had done the right thing in going to Rome in the first place, or if leaving the priesthood was a terrible thing. I told myself it was better not to think about that.

Often one learns to see oneself in a new way through the eyes of another. A few years later, someone in California said, "I think the fact that you were a priest is wonderful and I actually feel honored to know you. You've been able to experience life in ways that not many people are able to. And you could do a lot of good for people in so many ways. What a great gift to have lived in the seminary in Rome, to have been a priest! And now you're here, part of my life!"

This helped me to stop being ashamed of my past, and to accept and embrace it. Learning to be true to myself, no longer to project an imaginary person, helped me to build closer and more meaningful relationships. What I could offer others was not a heart torn and needing to cling in order to feel whole. Instead I had a new, still imperfect, capacity to love without needing the other to complete what was lacking in me.

I soon discovered what it meant to fall in love. "Friends are like one soul in two bodies," Aristotle wrote. Instead of the torment of need there was the peace of fulfillment, since the love of the other did not take the place of the love of myself. To truly love was to give myself to the other, not to replace myself with the other.

What I had learned in the CF Movement in Rome, in my years in the priesthood and in the process of disengaging, were all part of this thing called my life and I didn't have to give up anything. I would always carry the experience of the movement, always seeking that infinite object of my deepest questions and longings. In the priesthood, my life was imbued with purpose and meaning so that I could never be satisfied with living a trivial existence. The difficult process of leaving showed me the value of inner strength, never to be the victim. My life since has shown me that I can love myself and my life the way God loves me. This unconditional embrace is that entry point in which the door of my heart could open towards others. The human and the Divine were no longer at war.

It was evening as we went silently up the path on the Janiculum hill, walking past the North American College. Near the summit we paused at the small outdoor bar where I had sometimes come for a coffee when I was a seminarian.

"How do you feel," my friend Mike asked, as we continued on the road overlooking Rome, "seeing these sights from your past: the seminary, the Vatican over there, the university where you took classes? Are you okay with all of this?"

We stopped. I gazed at the Coliseum, the dome of St. Peter's, the ancient buildings and churches, and above them, the glowing sky filled with stars.

"I feel . . . happy."